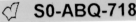
TRAVELLERS

EGYPT

By
MICHAEL HAAG

Written by Michael Haag
Updated by Cheryl Wynne-Eyton

Original photography by Rick Strange

Editing and page layout by Cambridge Publishing Management Ltd,
Unit 2, Burr Elm Court, Caldecote CB23 7NU
Series Editor: Rosalind Munro

Published by Thomas Cook Publishing
A division of Thomas Cook Tour Operations Ltd
Company Registration No. 1450464 England

PO Box 227, The Thomas Cook Business Park
Coningsby Road, Peterborough PE3 8SB, United Kingdom
E-mail: books@thomascook.com
www.thomascookpublishing.com
Tel: +44(0)1733 416477

ISBN: 978-1-84157-803-3

Text © 2007 Thomas Cook Publishing
Maps © 2007 Thomas Cook Publishing
First edition © 2002 Thomas Cook Publishing
Second edition © 2005 Thomas Cook Publishing
Third edition © 2007 Thomas Cook Publishing

Project Editor: Kelly Anne Pipes
Production/DTP Editor: Steven Collins

Printed and bound in Italy by: Printer Trento.

Front cover credits: © Thomas Cook, © Thomas Cook, © Thomas Cook
Back cover credits: © Thomas Cook, © Gavin Hellier/Alamy

Contents

KEY TO MAPS

Ⓜ	Metro station
★	Start of walk/tour
—	Approximate route of new road
∨∨	City walls/fortifications
✈	Airport
▲ 2285m	Mountain
𝒊	Tourist information

4

Introduction

Pervaded with an impressive sense of permanence and duration, Egypt is an eternal amalgam of two elements: the constancy of the Nile and the labours of its people. Five thousand years of history have been fashioned from these givens. Like the gigantic bird migrations that sweep up the valley, storming foreigners (Persian, Greek, Arab, Turkish, British) have passed across Egypt in magnificent spectacle, but in their wake the country has remained essentially unchanged. Egyptians are warm, friendly and generous, ambitious, intelligent, religious and proud. Above all, they are open, and sometimes so insistent that the first-time visitor is likely to be confused, his reactions and emotions swinging like a pendulum. Yet, if you can take the pace, the sheer vitality of the Egyptian people becomes a wonderful roller-coaster ride, guaranteed to brighten your visit.

'About Egypt I shall have a great deal more to relate because of the number of remarkable things which the country contains, and because of the fact that more monuments which beggar description are to be found there than anywhere in the world.'

HERODOTUS
The Histories, c.430 BC

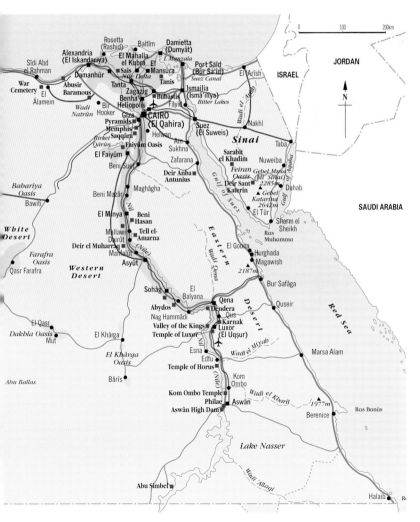

Land and people

Covering a total area of 1,002,000sq km (386,874sq miles), Egypt occupies the extreme northeast corner of the African continent, and the Sinai peninsula, which is in Asia. It is bounded to the west by Libya, to the south by Sudan, to the east by the Red Sea and Israel, and to the north by the Mediterranean.

Central and southern Sinai is mountainous, its peaks ranging from 750m to 1,500m (2,460ft to 4,920ft), though Gebel Musa (Mount Sinai) rises to 2,285m (7,497ft), and the summit of Gebel Katarina, the highest mountain in Egypt, is 2,642m (8,668ft). The mountain range running down the mainland's Red Sea coast is between 350m and 750m (1,150ft and 2,460ft) high. Otherwise, Egypt is a low, flat country, the Western Desert averaging 200m (650ft) above sea level, while the Nile falls only 87m (285ft) in its journey of some 1,000km (620 miles) northwards from Aswân to the Mediterranean sea. North of Cairo the river divides in two, its arms passing through the Delta and debouching into the sea at Rashid (Rosetta) and Dumyât (Damietta).

About 10,000 years ago a dramatic change in climate caused the once fertile lands of northern Africa and the Middle East to turn to dust, and their people migrated to the few remaining riverine areas. The Nile provided water, and its annual flood covered the valley with rich alluvial soil. But the river had to be regulated, swamps drained, canals dug, fields planted and irrigated – an entire complex system maintained. To this task Egypt's peasants, the *fellahin*, gave their labour, and the state provided direction.

Upper and Lower Egypt

Though it sometimes confuses the modern traveller to find Upper Egypt at the bottom of the map and Lower Egypt at the top, Memphis, the ancient capital just south of present-day Cairo, was deliberately sited to exercise a united authority over the upriver valley land (Upper Egypt), and the downriver Delta land (Lower Egypt).

The ancient Egyptians felicitously likened their united land to a lotus plant. The river valley was the stem, the Faiyûm the bud, the delta the flower. Yet this slender figure of fertility covers less than 10 per cent of modern Egypt's total area, and within it lives 95 per cent of the nation's population, its density one of the highest in the world. The rest of the country is desert, where only a few Bedouin and oasis-dwellers can survive.

Apart from its Mediterranean coastline, where Alexandria enjoys an annual rainfall of 184mm (7^1/$_4$in), Egypt is exceptionally arid. Cairo receives only 24mm (1in) of rain a year, while the rest of the country receives less than even 10mm (^{1}/$_2$in). Without the Nile, aptly known as the River of Life, there could be no agriculture in Egypt.

The Nile

Until the completion of the High Dam at Aswân in 1971, all life in Egypt depended on the annual rise and fall of the Nile. The river fell throughout the winter months, reaching its lowest level in May. In June it began to rise again, reaching its peak in September. The rising Nile, which came at precisely the driest and hottest time in the Egyptian year, was caused by spring and summer rains in the African interior. The inundation also brought with it millions of tons of mineral-rich sediment.

The Nile has now backed up behind the High Dam to create Lake Nasser. Capable of holding several times more water than Egypt's annual requirement, the lake ensures a steady year-round flow from one year to the next, and so protects the country from Africa's droughts and famines.

There are ecological drawbacks, however, including the dependence on artificial fertilisers instead of silt. Also, the ancient land of Nubia, which stretched from the First Cataract at Aswân south into Sudan, has vanished beneath the lake. Most of the displaced Nubians, a distinct ethnic group, have been resettled around Kom Ombo, to the north of the dam.

Land and people

Bedouins and their camels stop for a much-needed break while traversing the Sinai desert

History

As you will discover when visiting a museum or a site, or when reading almost anything about ancient Egypt, it is the usual practice to date pharaohs, monuments and artefacts in terms of dynasties rather than by years. The system began with the ancient priests and has been adopted by Egyptologists. Additionally, Egyptologists – though not the ancient Egyptians themselves – have grouped the various dynasties into broader periods, for example, Old Kingdom and New Kingdom.

The royal dynasties of ancient Egypt

Priests traditionally recorded long lists of Egypt's monarchs, describing the key events during each pharaoh's reign. Most Egyptologists are in agreement that these recordings were done in stone, although some say that lists also exist in papyrus (one of them being in Italy). An example is the list of Seti I's predecessors at Abydos (*see p84*).

Working from such lists, Manetho, an Egyptian priest under the early Ptolemies, arranged all the rulers of Egypt from Menes to Alexander into 31 dynasties. His lists can be seen at the Karnak Temple in Luxor, and also in a tomb at Saqqâra.

Egyptologists have relied on Manetho's list and have been able to confirm its essential accuracy while sometimes improving upon it. The dates they have attached to the dynasties, however, are subject to varying margins of error, up to 100 years for the third millennium BC, around 10 years from 2000 BC onwards. Periods, dynasties and their dates are listed below, along with some of the more important pharaohs and events associated with them.

Relief carving at Tell el Amarna's rock tombs

First Dynastic Period 3100–2700 BC

1st Dynasty	3100–2800 BC Menes (Narmer) unites Upper and Lower Egypt; establishes Memphis as his capital.

2nd Dynasty	2800–2700 BC

Old Kingdom 2700–2200 BC

Period of stability.

3rd Dynasty	2700–2650 BC Zoser builds the Step Pyramid at Saqqâra.

4th Dynasty	2650–2500 BC Chephren, Cheops and Mycerinus build their pyramids at Gîza.

5th Dynasty	2500–2350 BC Saqqâra pyramid built.

6th Dynasty	2350–2200 BC

First Intermediate Period 2200–2000 BC

Collapse of central authority.

7th & 8th Dynasties	2180–2155 BC

9th & 10th Dynasties	2155–2055 BC

11th Dynasty	2055–2000 BC

Middle Kingdom 2000–1800 BC

Egypt reunited. Conquest of Nubia.

12th Dynasty	2000–1780 BC Major building works and hydrological programmes in the Faiyûm.

Second Intermediate Period 1800–1550 BC

Collapse of central authority.

13th–17th Dynasties	1780–1570 BC The alien Hyksos people rule in Lower Egypt from 1730–1570 BC. The chariot is introduced.

New Kingdom 1570–1090 BC

Period of power, luxury and cosmopolitanism.

18th Dynasty	1570–1305 BC Hyksos expelled; royal residence, political and religious capital at Thebes. Grandiose building works at Thebes and Karnak. *Tuthmosis I*, 1525–1495 BC, initiates burials in Valley of the Kings. *Hatshepsut*, 1486–1468 BC, is regent for, then co-ruler with, Tuthmosis III, whom she overshadows in her lifetime. Builds magnificent mortuary temple in Theban necropolis. *Tuthmosis III*, 1490–1436 BC, a great military leader, lays foundation for African and Asian empire.

Amenophis III, 1398–1361 BC. Apogee of New Kingdom opulence. *Amenophis IV* (Akhenaton), 1369–1353 BC, opposes priesthood of Amun; moves capital to Tell el Amarna; establishes worship of the Aton. His queen is Nefertiti. *Tutankhamun*, 1352–1344 BC. Return to the worship of Amun.

19th Dynasty
1305–1200 BC
Seti I, 1302–1290 BC, revives Old Kingdom style. *Ramses II*, 1290–1224 BC Prodigious builder, for example, the Ramesseum and Abu Simbel.

20th Dynasty
1200–1090 BC
Egypt enters the Iron Age. *Ramses III*, 1195–1164 BC, defeats Sea Peoples; he is the last great pharaoh.

Late Dynastic Period 1090–332 BC
Period of decline; often foreign rule.

21st Dynasty
1090–945 BC
Capital at Tanis.

22nd Dynasty
945–745 BC
Libyan origin.

23rd Dynasty
745–718 BC
Ethiopian kings control Upper Egypt.

24th Dynasty
718–712 BC. Ethiopian kings control the whole of Egypt.

25th Dynasty
712–663 BC
Taharka, an Ethiopian king, builds First Pylon at Karnak; defeated by Assyrians; sack of Thebes.

26th Dynasty
663–525 BC
Delta rulers, their capital at Sais; Assyrians ejected with Greek help. *Necho*, 610–595 BC, attempts to link Red Sea and Mediterranean by canal. Circumnavigation of Africa.

27th Dynasty
525–404 BC
Persian rule.

28th Dynasty
404–399 BC
Persians ejected with Greek help.

29th Dynasty
399–380 BC
Delta remains centre of power.

30th Dynasty
380–343 BC
Nectanebos I, 380–343 BC, builds at Philae.

31st Dynasty
343–332 BC
Persian rule. Alexander the Great makes Egypt part of his empire in 332 BC.

323–282 BC *Ptolemy I Soter*, one of Alexander's generals, makes himself king of Egypt and establishes the Ptolemaic dynasty that rules the country to the death of Cleopatra in 30 BC. He founds the Mouseion with its Library at Alexandria, which, like the Ptolemies themselves, is Greek in culture. Upriver, the Ptolemies preserve the old-style pharaonic architecture and religion.

282–246 BC *Ptolemy II Philadelphos* builds the Pharos in Alexandria.

246–221 BC *Ptolemy III Euergetes* builds at Karnak; begins temple of Edfu.

221–205 BC *Ptolemy IV Philopator* begins temples at Esna and Kom Ombo.

80–51 BC *Ptolemy XII Neos Dionysos* staves off Roman annexation. Builds at Dendera, Edfu and Philae.

51–30 BC *Cleopatra VII*. Her policy is to preserve Egyptian power by joining forces with Rome. Through Julius Caesar, and then Mark Antony, she nearly succeeds.

30 BC Octavian (later Augustus Caesar) captures Alexandria. Cleopatra and Antony commit suicide; Egypt becomes a Roman province.

AD 45 According to legend, St Mark introduces Christianity to Egypt.

249–251 Reign of Decius; severe Christian persecutions.

251–356 Life of St Antony, the world's first hermit.

284–305 Reign of Diocletian. His accession marks the beginning of the 'Era of Martyrs', the persecutions from which the Copts date their calendar.

313 Edict of Milan, tolerating Christianity.

About 330 Founding of the world's first monasteries, at Wadi Natrûn.

379–395 Reign of Theodosius I. He declares Christianity the official religion of the Roman Empire, which is now partitioned. Egypt is ruled from Constantinople, capital of the East Roman (Byzantine) Empire.

451   Council of Chalcedon declares the monophysite Egyptian (Coptic) Church heretical.

476   Fall of the Roman Empire in the West.

622   Mohammed's flight from Mecca, the *hegira*, from which the Muslim calendar is reckoned.

640   Arab invasion of Egypt. Babylon (Old Cairo) falls in 641; Alexandria surrenders in 642.

878   Ibn Tulun, Abbassid governor of Egypt, makes himself independent of the Abbassid caliphate at Baghdad.

969   Cairo founded by Fatimids who invade Egypt from North Africa.

971   El Azhar founded.

1099   Crusaders take Jerusalem.

1171   Saladin founds his Ayyubid dynasty in Egypt; fortifies the Citadel. He recaptures Jerusalem in 1187.

1250–1517   Egypt ruled by Mameluke sultans, whose great builders include Qalaun (1279–90), Hassan (1347–61), Qaytbay (1469–95) and El Ghuri (1500–1516).

Early 1300s   Severe persecution of the Copts, still half the population of Egypt; mass conversions to Islam follow.

1517   Egypt becomes part of the Ottoman Empire.

1798–1801   French occupation.

1805–49   Mohammed Ali makes himself master of Egypt. Begins modernisation, refounds Alexandria and establishes dynasty which lasts until Nasser's revolution.

1869   Opening of the Suez Canal.

1882   Nationalist uprising against Turkish and European influence. British occupy Egypt.

1936   Anglo-Egyptian Treaty, formally ending British

occupation of Egypt, except for Canal Zone.

1939–45 British army re-enters Egypt to repel Italians and Germans. Rommel defeated at El Alamein in 1942.

1948 British leave Palestine; creation of state of Israel. Arab-Israeli war.

1952 Army officers led by Nasser stage coup; King Farouk abdicates.

1956 Nasser nationalises the Suez Canal; Israel, France and Britain invade Egypt, but withdraw after international protest.

Feluccas have been sailing the Nile since antiquity

1967 Israel attacks and defeats Egypt in the 'Six-Day War', and occupies Sinai.

1970 Nasser dies; Sadat becomes president.

1971 Completion of the Aswân High Dam.

1973 October War; Egyptian army crosses the canal.

1977 Sadat visits Jerusalem in dramatic peace bid.

1981 Sadat assassinated by Muslim fundamentalists. Hosni Mubarak becomes president.

1982 Israel evacuates Sinai.

1984–98 Political and economic liberalisation, but also a rise in Islamic conservatism.

2005–2006 In a surprise move, in February President Hosni Mubarak asks Parliament to alter the constitution so that a range of candidates can stand for president.

2007 President Mubarak says he will stay on as president.

Politics

The Arab Republic of Egypt (ARE), to give Egypt its official title, has its capital at Cairo. Its chief executive is the president, who is elected for a six-year term. He determines the country's policies, is head of the armed forces, and he nominates the vice-president, the prime minister, and other high political, civil and military officials.

The People's Assembly, all but 10 of its 454 members elected by popular vote for a five-year term, is the legislative body, advised by the Consultative Assembly, which functions only in an advisory capacity. The Constitution guarantees freedom of religion and thought, declares Islam to be the official religion of the state, and announces that the principles of Islamic law (*Sharia*) constitute the inspiring fount of legislation.

In the pyramid of the Egyptian state, however, the summit imposes itself on the base. Freedom of the press is increasing and there are now several independent publications, but it is still undermined by sycophancy. Although it has been reported that free elections could take place, with everybody eligible to run, this is somewhat misleading. Elections are nominally under judicial supervision and, in reality, are heavily biased towards the National Democratic Party.

Nasser's legacy

The country is still burdened by Nasser's legacy. Whatever his nationalist ideals, he was a dictator whose socialist policies helped wreck the economy. Before the deposition of King Farouk in 1952, education accounted for more than 12 per cent of government spending, and defence, under 10 per cent. Defence now eats about 30 per cent, while education receives only 6 per cent, although change is afoot. Pre-revolutionary Egypt was self-sufficient in food, and its foreign exchange reserves were US $25 billion in today's terms, but now it must import a high proportion of its food. It has a national (domestic) debt of over US $33 billion and, were it not for the income from tourism, the Suez Canal, oil and particularly gas, the economy would collapse.

There have been some improvements, but the yawning gap between rich and poor still remains. Under the monarchy the 2,000 richest people owned as much land as the 1.5 million peasants. Nothing has changed. Over 70,000 Egyptians own Mercedes cars, or similar, each one worth the lifetime salary of a factory worker.

Recent developments

After the revolution in 1952, nearly a quarter of a million foreigners, most of them highly skilled, were forced to leave. In recent years more than three million Egyptians have followed in their footsteps, seeking opportunities in the Gulf and the West, but this figure has decreased somewhat. Immigration is still an attractive option for Egyptians trying to make a better life abroad, but Iraq is now closed and the Gulf states are taking fewer and fewer Egyptians in favour of other nationalities.

A real effort is being made to renovate the once-beautiful cities of Cairo and Alexandria, but stretches of the north and Red Sea coasts have fallen victim to unplanned growth. Attention is being paid to newer developments there and resorts such as El Gouna in order to avoid similar mistakes.

The population now stands at about 75 million, and increases by one million every nine months, outstripping land reclamation, food production and the creation of new jobs. The need for birth control apart, the government has belatedly removed some of the subsidies on foodstuffs although transportation, petrol and gas are still heavily subsidised. Poverty has

increased, with inflation very high at around 11 per cent. There is still massive unemployment and, more specifically, underemployment, with a desperate need to improve social services, including health care, water, transportation and education. However, despite stifling bureaucracy, private enterprise is being encouraged. But sudden reforms could further impoverish the poor and cause massive job losses and political unrest. Anxiety and discontent have been exploited in the past by Islamic fundamentalism.

Egypt has gone through a very tough and challenging period. Now, with a great push for foreign direct investment, ample resources of water, land, oil and gas, unparalleled tourist attractions and an ideal location for trade, the country also enjoys considerable advantages upon which to build a bright future.

THOMAS COOK'S EGYPT

Egypt is the country most closely associated with the history of Thomas Cook. Cook was invited to the opening of the Suez Canal in 1869 and opened an office in Cairo. He was nearly drowned on his first Nile excursion, but survived to become owner of a fleet of 40 Nile cruisers. As the sole agent for mail and passenger traffic in Egypt, he was largely responsible for creating the booming tourist trade the country knows today. In 1884, when General Gordon was besieged by the Mahdi in Khartoum, Cook was asked to provide the transport for an Anglo-Egyptian force of 30,000 men and 100,000 tons of stores.

Religion

Until the Arab invasion in ad 641, Egypt was a Christian country, but within 500 years the majority of Egyptians had become Muslims. About ten per cent of the population, however, have remained Christian, and are called Copts, a corruption of the Greek word for Egypt, Aigyptos. *There are no physical differences between Copts and Muslims. Nor do they differ in language or culture. Both groups are proud to call themselves Egyptians, and live harmoniously together.*

Christians

St Mark is the legendary 1st-century founder of Christianity in Egypt. From its earliest roots among the Jews and Greeks of Alexandria, Christianity soon spread among the native population, where it resonated with such ancient Egyptian notions as resurrection and the afterlife. Isis and the infant Horus, for example, resemble the Virgin and Child, and it was no accident that a native-born Egyptian theologian of Alexandria first pronounced Mary to be the Mother of God. Monasticism also began in Egypt and went on to make a profound spiritual impact on the world.

By the 5th century, the Roman and Byzantine empires had split, and Egypt was ruled from Constantinople. Soon a theological argument, abetted by nationalist undercurrents, developed. In Constantinople and Rome, it was held that Christ had two separate natures, the human and the divine. However, Alexandrian theologians, while admitting the two natures, emphasised their unity. For this they were called monophysites (believers in only one nature), and were charged with heresy at the Ecumenical Council of Chalcedon in 451, resulting in their break from Rome.

Had national pride not got in the way, the theological differences might have been overcome. But at the moment of the Arab invasion, Egypt was in a state of mutiny against the Byzantine Empire, whose forces could do nothing but abandon the country. Over the centuries the Coptic Church

COPTIC CHURCH

Orthodox Coptic rituals include fasting and conducting the Mass, with 30 per cent of the prayers still in the Coptic language. The Coptic *Deskilia* – a book of teachings said to have been handed down from St Mark to the Coptic Orthodox Church – is still used.

was forced to turn in upon itself, and preserved ancient rituals while failing to develop. It is now, however, experiencing a renaissance and has a flourishing congregation, while, in a new ecumenical spirit, links are being forged with Christian churches worldwide.

Muslims

Of the two predominant Muslim sects, Sunni and Shia, Egypt's Muslims are Sunnis. Unlike the Shias who claimed that the Prophet's successor, the next Caliph, be appointed by virtue of heredity, the Sunnis advocated succession by democratic consensus.

Relief carving with Christian motif, Museum of Antiquities, Luxor

Islam

The principal belief of Islam is the existence of one God, the same God worshipped by Jews and Christians, known to all Arabs as Allah. Islam means submission. Muslim means one who submits to one God as interpreted by the Prophet Mohammed.

Mohammed was a merchant in Arabia. He often went to contemplate in the desert, and at the age of 40 he had a vision of the angel Gabriel who commanded him to proclaim monotheism to the pagan Arabian tribes. He did so, and the words of Allah as given to Mohammed became known as the Quran. Concerned by the unsettling effects of this new

Typical Islamic mosque decoration

The night skyline

religion, the merchants of Mecca drove Mohammed out of the city in 622.

His flight (known as the *hegira*) from Mecca to Medina, where Islam first took root, marks the start of the Islamic calendar.

In Islam, the one who believes and worships approaches God directly and simply. All Muslims must perform five practical devotions, the five Pillars of Faith. They must pronounce the fundamental creed: 'I bear witness that there is no god but Allah and Mohammed is his prophet'; pray five times a day; give part of their income to charity; fast during Ramadan; and make the pilgrimage (Haj) to Mecca.

The most visible of these devotions is prayer. A muezzin makes the call to prayer, usually by loudspeaker these days, from the minaret of a mosque. Prayer may take place in a mosque, at home, at the office or anywhere, but worshippers always prostrate themselves in the direction of Mecca.

Westerners will be struck by the extent to which Islam permeates all areas of public and private life. This follows from the Quran, which is as much a book of laws and rules of conduct to be observed in day to day living, as it is a spiritual guide. Indeed, within Islam, there is no separation of the secular and religious life.

Culture

Egyptian culture is Arabic, with something of an African feel. In Alexandria especially, and to a lesser extent in Cairo, there is additionally an atmosphere of the French, and of the Levant, with its amalgam of Greek, Turkish and Syrian cultures. Cairo itself is distinctly cosmopolitan.

Following the 7th-century AD Arab invasion, the new holders of power and patrons of culture spread the Arabic language and Islam which, with its prohibition on the depiction of human images, had a decisive effect in separating the greater part of Egypt's population from its pharaonic and Graeco-Roman past. The ancient inheritance only survives in a much transmuted form within the Coptic Church (*see p16*).

The outlook and lifestyle of Egypt's urban middle class are not dissimilar to those of people living in Europe and America. In Cairo, for example, with its many bookshops, cafés and cinemas, its Opera House, its cultural societies and universities, there is ample opportunity to share in and contribute to the broad international experience.

Life is a grind for the poor in the cities, though many willingly seek the slender promise of a better life here rather than endure the monotonous labour of the countryside, largely unchanged since pharaonic times. Relief is provided by television and the cinema, but also by such popular celebrations as *moulids*, which are the Egyptian equivalent of medieval saints' anniversaries and fairs. Here, booths sell crafts and sweets, and marriages are arranged. There is music, the hypnotic whirling of dervishes, puppet shows, storytellers and dancing.

The novels of Naguib Mahfouz, who won the Nobel Prize in 1989, offer a vivid portrait of modern Egypt's multi-faceted society.

A wandering Nubian musician

The bustle of daily life on the streets of the city

Festivals

Religious festivals, both Muslim and Christian, are often times of joyful public celebration. There is usually an atmosphere of infectious hospitality and bonhomie, and sometimes there is entertainment in the form of music and dancing, as well as special souks. Almost all Muslim festivals are fixed in accordance with the 12 lunar months of the Islamic calendar, which means that they do not occur on the same date each year. (See National Holidays, pp184–5.)

Ramadan

During this month of fasting, practised by all good Muslims, nothing is permitted to pass the lips between sunrise and sunset. As it happens, more food is consumed in Egypt during Ramadan than in any other month of the year, everyone more than making up at night for what they gave up during the day. The nights, therefore, take on something of a carnival atmosphere. This can be a good time to stroll the streets, which are lit by coloured lanterns, and thronged with animated crowds, often with singing and dancing in the squares and cafés. In Cairo it is especially worth going to the square in front of the Sayyidna Hussein Mosque in Khan el Khalili. At Luxor the festivities take place on the grass in front of the Mosque of Abu el Haggag at Luxor Temple.

ISLAMIC MONTHS

Moharram	1st month (30 days)
Safar	2nd month (29 days)
Rabei el Awal	3rd month (30 days)
Rabei el Tani	4th month (29 days)
Gamad el Awal	5th month (30 days)
Gamad el Tani	6th month (29 days)
Ragab	7th month (30 days)
Shaaban	8th month (29 days)
Ramadan	9th month (30 days)
Shawal	10th month (29 days)
Zoul Qidah	11th month (30 days)
Zoul Hagga	12th month (29 days, 30 in leap years)

Eid el Fitr

This three-day feast comes as a celebratory climax to Ramadan which it immediately follows. It is a time when families and friends come together.

Eid el Adha (Quarban Bairam)

This Great Feast, which celebrates Abraham's willingness to sacrifice Isaac, occurs from the 10th to the 13th of Zoul Hagga – the month when the Haj, or annual Pilgrimage, takes place.

Everyone who can afford to slaughters a sheep or a cow, and distributes a portion of it for the occasion to the poor and needy.

Ras el Sana el Hegira
The Islamic New Year begins on the first day of the month of Moharram. Quranic and other religious texts are read at this time.

Muslim and Christian moulids
A *moulid* is a festival in honour of a holy man and, its devotional aspects aside, it usually takes on the character of a medieval fair with popular entertainments and a souk.

The **Moulid el Nabi**, which is a nationwide Muslim celebration of the Prophet's birthday on the 12th day of Rabei el Awal, is marked in Cairo by a spectacular procession. The place to be is the square in front of the Sayyidna Hussein Mosque in Khan el Khalili.

Most *moulids*, however, are local affairs, albeit sometimes on a gigantic scale as at Tanta (*see p60*). The *moulid* of Abu el Haggag, whose mosque sits atop the walls of Luxor Temple, occurs on the 14th of Shaaban, and is one of the largest and wildest in Upper Egypt. During the week leading up to St Shenute's *moulid* on 14 July, thousands of people from all over Upper Egypt attend the sprawling encampment of tented stalls at the White Monastery outside Sohâg, where the night is filled with drifting laughter, the aroma of cooked foods, and the sinuous sound of Egyptian music.

Whirling Dervishes
Mevlana, the 13th-century Sufi master who founded his sect of Whirling Dervishes at Konya in Turkey, has his followers in Egypt. Suspect, and indeed often banned in other Muslim countries, their intention is to achieve mystical union with God through ecstatic whirling. On Wednesdays and Saturdays from 7.30pm to 9pm, they can be seen at the cultural centre inside the El Ghuri Mausoleum on Sharia Muizz, Cairo.

Sham el Nessim
This national holiday, with its roots in the Christian and pharaonic traditions, falls on the first Monday after Coptic Easter. All Egyptians, of whatever religion, take the day off to celebrate the advent of spring, usually by picnicking.

Lantern shops do a good trade selling lanterns for Ramadan

Impressions

Arriving in Egypt is like entering a bazaar. Your senses are invaded by its colour, its noise, its smells, its animation. Movement is eager, heaving, seemingly chaotic. Everything is thrust at you. Well, Egypt is something of a bazaar, and it is up to you how much you want to respond to what is on offer. At first you may feel overwhelmed and uncertain, but you are free to experience it at a relaxed pace. Nobody will mind if you take your time in getting the measure of the place.

Arabic

The language of Egypt is Arabic. It is written from right to left, using an alphabet of 29 letters. There is no completely satisfactory system for conveying the sound of Arabic letters in Western languages. Nor is there agreement on the transliteration of Egyptian place names. Therefore, Faiyûm might appear as Fayyum, Saqqâra as Sakkara, Dendera as Dendarah, and so on. This can present an even bigger problem when the initial letters vary; for example, Edfu instead of Idfu, or Qena instead of Kena. So do not rely entirely on spelling; instead, try

'It is not well to drink much wine, beer, or spirits in Egypt, but coffee may be far more freely indulged in than in Europe or America. As regards smoking, most men come down to cigarettes or mild tobacco in native pipes.'
Charles G Leland
The Egyptian Sketchbook, 1873

to think phonetically when looking for places on maps, signs, and in this guide.

For the sake of simplicity, El (or el) has been used throughout this guide, for example, El Azhar is used rather than Al Azhar (or al-Azhar). The Arabic for street is *sharia*, and for square it is *midan* – at least those are the spellings that are used here. These come before the name; for example, Sharia Ramses and Midan el Tahrir.

Inshallah, bukra and maalesh

Part of Egyptian tradition, though increasingly out of date in today's faster-moving Egypt, are three commonly heard words, *inshallah*, *bukra* and *maalesh*, whose meanings, and more importantly, whose nuances, you should know. Together they provide some insight into how things work, or frequently, do not work, in Egypt.

Inshallah means 'God willing', and, reasonably enough, it conveys the caution that even with the best of human intentions nothing can be certain, and everything is in the hands of Allah. However, it can also be a diplomatic way of saying that you cannot commit yourself, indeed, of even suggesting that the thing promised will not happen.

Bukra means 'tomorrow', but it would be a mistake to take this literally. *Bukra*, in fact, more usually refers to some indefinite point in time between tomorrow and never.

Maalesh can mean 'never mind', or 'it's all right'.

Baksheesh

The word *baksheesh* literally means 'share the wealth'. It is payable for all services, however small, and, as often as not, is expected for nothing at all. Alms-giving is a central tenet of Islam, and few Egyptians will balk at accepting their share. You have it, they do not, and so they feel you should pass it round.

Baksheesh is the tip you might give to the man who has carried your luggage. It is also the reward placed deftly in the outstretched hand of the guardian who lets you into a tomb after closing time, or given to the railway carriage attendant who discovers there is a sleeping compartment free after all. There may be times when you wish to give something out of charity – that, too, is *baksheesh*. But *baksheesh* can be a plague. Children may pester you

for it in the streets, or you may have paid but are pressed for more.

The basic rule is to offer *baksheesh* only in return for a service, and not to pay until the service has been performed, and also to resist firmly any attempt at intimidation.

The pace of life in Egypt can vary from relaxed, as here, to chaotic

Catching cold

When you think of Egypt you think of sun and heat, and so you will, of course, think of taking light clothes, sunglasses, and a hat or scarf to protect yourself against sunstroke. But that is not the whole of the story. You need to be aware of the extremes of temperature in Egypt, and that can mean extremes of cold as well as heat. The desert can be punishingly hot by day, but it can rapidly become chilly, and outside the summer months, cold, as soon as the sun goes down. Even attending the Sound and Light show at the Giza Pyramids on the edge of the desert can prove to be uncomfortably cool.

The same is true of the mountainous landscapes of Sinai and along the Red Sea coast – you could easily turn blue on top of Mount Sinai while waiting for the sun to rise. In the desert and the mountains you should carry a sweater with you at night, even in summer. (*For details of* Climate, *see pp177–8.*)

Living standards

The living standards of a great number of Egyptians are very low, and visitors may be distressed at the poverty they will sometimes encounter. Egyptians, however, are a proud people. Family and neighbourhood networks serve as a form of social security system. There is little homelessness here. Numerous people may pack into a room, or families may live among the tombs in Cairo's City of the Dead, but no one

SUPERSTITION

Superstition says that the envious glance of a passer-by, attracted by an immodest show of wealth, achievement or beauty, can harm or bewitch. Reciting certain verses of the Quran is one way of warding it off; the Eye of Horus is another. It may be painted on cars, trucks, and fishing boats, or worn as an amulet, particularly by children, who are especially vulnerable to the 'evil eye'. Therefore, it is a good idea not to admire something too much – your behaviour can be mistaken for desire, and you may find that you are presented with the object of your attention.

sleeps out on the street unless by choice. Outright begging is rare; the request for *baksheesh* usually supposes that some service has been performed. Your greatest contribution to the situation is to visit Egypt, for tourism creates jobs.

Manners and customs

Egyptian values are rooted in the strong family attachments of a still over-whelmingly rural heritage, and in Islam's closely woven social code. Though allowances are made for foreign idiosyncrasies, and Egyptians have a more relaxed attitude to dress and behaviour, a degree of conservatism is expected from you. Physicality should be muted, so that men and women should refrain from kissing and hugging in public, while generally it is a good idea not to show too much flesh. Except at resorts such as Sharm El Sheikh and Hurghada, where pretty much anything goes, women should not wear shorts, dresses or skirts that are too short, and both women and men should cover their shoulders.

Do not photograph an Egyptian without asking permission. For some people it is extremely offensive, while others, who might not have minded, will feel that you have taken a liberty. If you do ask first, people are often happy to be photographed, and indeed, the occasion can be a way of getting to know people. Egyptians can be sensitive about many scenes you might find picturesque but which to them portray poverty or backwardness. If someone asks you to desist, it is best to do so and look for another chance elsewhere. Militarily sensitive subjects – including airports, railway stations, dams, bridges and government offices – should definitely not be photographed.

During the month of Ramadan, Muslims may not eat, drink or smoke while the sun is up. It would be polite if you, too, refrained, in public at least.

If you are invited to someone's home, it is customary to bring a gift, such as pastries or other local sweets.

Practical dress is a necessity

Reading the signs

The Arabic alphabet is completely different from that of other languages, but in general, street signs and all other notices relevant to the tourist will also be written in English, or sometimes French. You may soon come to recognise one word, however, which you will frequently see not only in mosques, but on the walls of shops, restaurants, almost anywhere – the Arabic for Allah:

You should make an effort to learn the Arabic numerals (from which Western numerals have derived – *see above right*). This will help you identify numbered buses and railway carriages, and understand prices.

Hieroglyphs

Hieroglyphs began in around 3000 BC as picture writing; the pictures conveyed an idea or story. Soon a phonetic alphabet of 24 letters was introduced, and if these only had been used, reading hieroglyphs would be easy. However, the priests also used more than 700 signs representing syllables. There are books available explaining how to read those symbols which are more common.

A distinctive feature of hieroglyphs is the cartouche, a stylised loop of rope which always encloses the name of a ruler, thereby conveying the idea of unending, unbroken power. In the 1820s, Jean François Champollion guessed that cartouches enclosed the names of rulers. When he saw some cartouches on the Rosetta Stone, then saw repeated below these, in Greek, the names of several rulers, he was able to match Greek letters to hieroglyphic symbols (*see p126*).

K L I O P A D R A

A cartouche containing Cleopatra's name

Numerals

·	١	٢	٣	٤	٥	٦	٧	٨	٩
0	1	2	3	4	5	6	7	8	9

The crown

Pharaohs are always shown wearing a crown, either the White Crown of Upper Egypt, or the Red Crown of Lower Egypt. The two are often combined to indicate the pharaoh's authority over a united Egypt. At the front of the crown is the *uraeus*, a hooded cobra, to ward off his enemies.

Philae, showing the combined crown of Egypt

Relief carving in the Temple of Hathor

Security

Egypt is a safe country for visitors. You are far safer walking through the streets of Cairo, where muggings are virtually unheard of, than through those of many European or American cities – and that is true both day and night.

There is a strong sense of communal responsibility, especially towards foreigners. Anyone in distress can expect the immediate assistance of both the public and the police.

In addition to the regular Metropolitan Police, who wear black uniforms in winter, white uniforms in summer, and who mostly speak only Arabic, there are special police who wear the same uniform but with a red armband saying 'Tourist Police'. They sometimes speak a foreign language, usually English (not necessarily at all fluently, however), and are posted at tourist sights, museums, airports, railway stations and ports. They are there to help if you are experiencing difficulties.

There are also the more soldierly-looking Central Security Police, always in black and armed with automatic weapons, who guard embassies, banks, post offices and other public buildings. A few fundamentalist fanatics who would like to turn Egypt into a theocratic Islamic state have attempted in the past to attack the government, and indeed the economy of the country, through tourism. By threatening and frightening away

Egyptian police in summer uniform

foreign visitors, their hope has been to destroy a major source of Egypt's income. Egyptians are, however, overwhelmingly opposed to such outrages, and the government has responded with determination, but, as in London or New York, it is never entirely possible to guarantee the elimination of terrorist activity. What can be said is that Egyptians remain a warm, good-humoured and hospitable people who care about the welfare of visitors to their country.

Tourists

You do not actually need to be a tourist to be called one. Egyptians, usually touts, generally call a foreigner, whether male or female, *khawaga*! This is the term applied to a foreigner, or a tourist, and also conveys the idea that you will have lots of money which you are about to spend (*see* Baksheesh, *p25*).

Touts

Touts are most common and relentless at the obvious tourist places, such as the Pyramids at Gîza, or along the corniche at Luxor. A polite but firm *la shukran* ('no thank you') should be enough to turn away unwanted attentions. If forced to rudeness, then *imshee* ('get lost') has the almost physical effect of a slap in the face. However, a kinder way to deter touts would be to say *sebne* ('leave me') or, if you can manage it, *sebne, lao samat* ('excuse me, leave me').

Do not assume that everyone is out to take advantage of you. People are often simply curious and some will be genuinely helpful.

Visiting mosques and monasteries

In visiting mosques and Christian monasteries, you are entering into the most conservative areas of Egyptian life, and therefore should take special care to dress and act with decorum. Shorts or short skirts should not be worn, nor should shoulders be bare, despite the fact that some nationalities pay scant heed to this. Inside mosques you must remove your shoes, or shoe coverings will be provided. For this, or if you accept the services of a guide, or ask to be shown the way up a minaret, *baksheesh* will be expected in addition to any entry fee.

You may sometimes find yourself in a mosque at prayer time. Then, although visitors are otherwise welcome, you may be asked to retreat into an alcove or out onto the street.

Except for St Catherine's Monastery in Sinai, which is Greek Orthodox, all Egyptian monasteries are Coptic. The Copts go in for a good deal of fasting, and during such periods their monasteries are closed to visitors. Please note, most mosques and churches will provide covering if necessary, with the exception of St Catherine's Monastery where no one incorrectly dressed will be admitted. (*For further details, see p178.*)

Shoe rack outside a mosque – you must remove your footwear before entering

Women travellers

Westerners going to Egypt are, to some extent, putting themselves in a position of contrast to the conventions of social life there, although in major tourist destinations a Western woman may never feel the cultural differences.

An Egyptian woman's life is very much bound up, indeed bounded, by her family relationships, whether as daughter, wife or mother. The entwined moral, religious and legal systems of the country enforce this. Middle- and lower-class educated women appear circumspect in their relationship with a man. Both families would be involved and the girl would be accompanied when in public situations. More affluent Egyptian women have all the appearance of a modern, Western female, often in dress and manner.

Your Western view may be that that is their business and your business is your own. Some Egyptians will make the effort to see it that way, especially as you are only passing through. A great many more will not agree.

Things in Egypt are, however, changing in two directions. In certain areas of Cairo and other cosmopolitan places such as the seaside resort of Sharm El Sheikh, women behave much like Westerners when it comes to dressing and having a good time. However, recently there has been a move afoot to revert to a more conservative way of life, at least outwardly. If wandering off the beaten tourist track and you have any doubt, dress conservatively.

If it helps, wear a wedding ring. Or keep in the company of other women,

Women mix freely with men in the market of Khan el Khalili

for example, when travelling on a train. If using the metro in Cairo, there are 'Ladies only' carriages, which are worth using. Egyptian women will happily adopt you into their circle.

There is no reason for you to put up with unwelcome attention. If, at worst, you are touched up, you can first say *imshee*, which means 'get lost'. If something stronger is called for, shout *sebne le wahadee*, which means 'leave me alone'. People will come to your aid, and the man will be so ashamed, he will probably run away.

El Azhar mosque in Cairo, the leading centre of Islamic theological teaching in the world

Cairo

Cairo is not only the largest city in Africa, but also the political and cultural pivot of the Arab world. Its population of around 17 million, swelling to 19 million on a daily basis, has grown five-fold within a generation, as fellahin *(Egypt's peasantry) have poured in from the countryside in search of opportunities. New bridges, flyovers and an excellent metro system keep the city from grinding to a halt, and there is constant new building.*

The most modern part of the city lies close to the Nile, which breathes through Cairo like a giant lung. Further east, towards the Moqattam Hills, is the medieval city of splendid mosques and thronging bazaars, founded by the Fatimids in AD 969. To the south is the now ruinous Fustat, the earliest Arab settlement, built when the Arabs invaded Egypt around AD 641. Westwards, beyond the sprawl of Gîza, the Pyramids glow gold at sundown against the Western Desert as they have done for thousands of years.

Abu Sarga Church (St Sargius)
See p47.
Old Cairo (Miṣr el Qadima). 4.5km (2 ³/4 miles) south of Midan el Tahrir. Open: 8am–4pm. Free admission. Metro: Mari Girgis.

Aqueduct
Much of the 3.5km- (2¹/4-mile-) long Mameluke aqueduct (AD 1505), which once brought water from the Nile to the Citadel, still survives. You can see it opposite the midpoint of Roda Island.

El Azhar Mosque
The El Azhar ('the most blooming') was completed in AD 971, the first mosque built by the Fatimids in their new city of Cairo. The world's foremost centre of Islamic theological teaching, it is also the oldest university in the world, with modern schools of medicine, science and languages nearby.

Although much rebuilt in a confusion of styles, the overall impression is of harmony, the atmosphere venerable. Off the central court, theological teachers sit, surrounded by their students, as was done a thousand years ago. There are

'You can never in your thoughts detach the Egypt of the past from the Egypt of today; neither, indeed, can you ever quite exclude it from sight.'
Howard Hopley
Under Egyptian Palms,
London, 1869

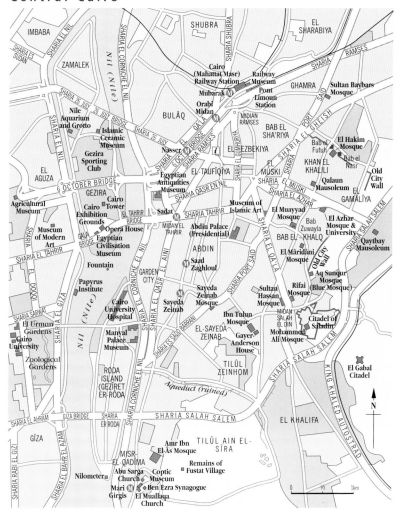

wonderful views of the medieval city
from the roof and minarets.

*Sharia el Azhar. 3km (1 ³/4 miles) east of
Midan el Tahrir. Open: winter, daily
9am–4pm; summer 9am–5pm. Closed:
11am–1pm during Friday prayers.
Admission charge.*

Bab Zuwayla, Bab el Futuh and
Bab el Nasr

The three surviving gates to the Fatimid
city (*see p44*).

Near the gates is the Khan el Khalili area of
bazaars (*see p38 and p44*).

Bayt el Suhaymi

This merchant's house of the Ottoman period, built during the 16th and 17th centuries, and completely furnished from that time, is the finest house in Cairo, and a wonderful example of Islamic secular architecture. Beautifully decorated rooms include the men's dining loggia, and the women's harem with its own private chapel and bathhouse, and bedrooms screened with intricately patterned *mashrabiyya* windows. Arranged around a garden courtyard, the dwelling is always deliciously cool.

Haret el Darb el Asfar, east of Sharia el Muizz. 3km (1³/4 miles) east of Midan el Tahrir. Open: 9am–4pm. Admission charge.

Ben Ezra Synagogue

See p47.
Old Cairo (Misr el Qadima). Open: daily 9am–4pm. Free admission. Metro: Mari Girgis.

Cairo Tower

Rising like a giant lotus 187m (613ft) above the island of Gezira, the tower's open observation platform and enclosed café and restaurant offer spectacular, panoramic views of the city.

Sharia el Burg el Qahira, towards the southern end of Gezira Island. 1km

Mohammed Ali Mosque at the Citadel overlooks the entire city of Cairo

(²/₃ mile) west of Midan el Tahrir. Open: 9am–midnight. Admission charge.

The Citadel

In 1176 Salah al-Din built his fortress on this spur of the Moqattam Hills above Cairo. For almost 700 years, to the death of Mohammed Ali in 1849, nearly all Egypt's rulers lived in the Citadel, held court, dispensed justice and received ambassadors (*see p43*). *The Citadel overlooks Midan Salah el Din, 3km (2 miles) southeast of Midan el Tahrir. Open: 9am–4pm. Closed: Friday 11.30am–1pm. Admission charge. The Carriage and Military Museums are extra.*

Bijou Palace

Mohammed Ali's palace, with its French-style salons, is now a museum of 19th-century royal portraits, sumptuous costumes and furnishings.

Citadel museums

See p40.

El Nasr Mohammed Mosque

Built during the early 14th century by the Mameluke Sultan el Nasr Mohammed, the marble panelling and much of the faïence decoration of the exterior were long ago stripped away, creating an austere impression. The arcades around the central courtyard, however, remain elegant in their proportions, their columns taken from ancient pharaonic, Roman and Byzantine buildings.

Mohammed Ali Mosque

A Turkish delight on the Cairo skyline, the mosque was built in imitation of the Ottoman imperial mosques of Istanbul. Half domes rise as buttresses for the high central dome, while two thin minarets add an ethereal touch. Mohammed Ali's tomb is on the right as you enter the vast and opulently decorated interior. From the courtyard outside, pollution permitting, there is a superb view of the city.

Gayer-Anderson House

Named after a British major who restored and occupied what is in fact two 17th-century houses knocked together, the house is filled with his eclectic collection of English, French and oriental furniture and bric-a-brac, giving the place a lived-in feel. The large reception room is overlooked by a balcony enclosed by a *mashrabiyya* (a screen through which the women of the harem could discreetly observe male visitors). *Abuts the Ibn Tulun Mosque off Sharia el Salibah, 500m (¹/₃ mile) west of the Citadel. 3km (2 miles) southeast of Midan el Tahrir. Tel: (202) 3647822. Open: 9am–4pm. Closed: Fri 11am–1.30pm. Admission charge.*

El Ghuri Wakala

El Ghuri Wakala, from the Mameluke period, was originally a merchants' hostel and warehouse. It now serves as workshops for artisans and sells Bedouin crafts (*see p44*).

Sharia Mohammed Abduh, near El Azhar Mosque. 3km (1³/₄ miles) east of Midan el Tahrir. Tel: (202) 5107146. Open: 9am–4pm. Closed: Fri. Admission charge for the exhibition area.

Ibn Tulun Mosque

One of the oldest and finest mosques in Cairo (*see p42*).

Off Sharia el Salibah, 500m (¹/₃ mile) west of the Citadel. 3km (1³/₄ miles) southeast of Midan el Tahrir. Open: 8am–6pm. Admission charge.

Khan el Khalili

The wealth of Cairo was built on trade, and from all over Africa and Asia, caravans would disgorge their cargoes for sale at the numerous bazaars that make up Khan el Khalili. Much of that medieval atmosphere still survives among the narrow covered passageways where you can join the throngs of Cairenes who bargain over spices and perfume, oils, gold and silver jewellery, leather goods and fabrics (*see p44*).

Within the northeast angle of Sharias el Muizz and el Muski, and spilling beyond as well. 3km (1³/₄ miles) east of Midan el Tahrir. Activity continues well on into the night. Most shops are closed on Sundays.

Manyal Palace

Built in 1903 for Prince Mohammed Ali, brother of the Khedive Abbas II, this oriental, rococo-style palace, set in a garden of banyan trees on Roda Island, is worth visiting for the opulence of its decoration and royal mementoes. The

THE MAMELUKES

As you walk through the streets of medieval Cairo (*see pp44–5*), you can still experience the atmosphere of *The Thousand and One Nights*. The tales were set in 9th-century Baghdad, but in reality they portray Cairo during the turbulent and spectacular Mameluke period (1250–1517).

The Mamelukes began as a slave militia, but they soon became an indispensable military elite who overthrew Salah el Din's dynasty. The Mamelukes saved Egypt from the Mongols and finished the task of driving the Crusaders from the Holy Land. Ruthless for power and often brutal, they nevertheless enriched Cairo with their bold and extravagant architecture, decorating its surfaces with intricate motifs and graceful arabesques. The mosque of Sultan Hassan and the mausoleum of Qaytbay are the two finest monuments from Mameluke times.

display includes a 1,000-piece silver service, a stuffed hermaphrodite goat, and a unique table made of elephants' ears. At the time of writing, certain sections of the palace are closed for renovation.

Sharia Ahmed Abdel Rahim, Roda Island. 2km (1¹/₄ miles) south of Midan el Tahrir. Tel: (202) 3687495. Open: 9am–4pm. Closed: Fri 11.30am–1pm. Admission charge.

El Muallaqa Church

This is popularly known as the Hanging Church because it is built on beams lying across the two walls of the Roman fortress (*see pp46–7*).

Old Cairo (Masr el Qadima). 4.5km (2³/₄ miles) south of Midan el Tahrir. Open: 8am–4pm. Free admission. Metro: Mari Girgis.

Nilometer

The 9th-century Nilometer, a graduated column, measured the rise and fall of the Nile, and was built to determine what the size of the harvest would be, and thus what taxes should be imposed. *Southern tip of Roda Island. 4.5km (3 miles) south of Midan el Tahrir. Open: 9am–4pm. Closed: Fri. Admission charge.*

Qaytbay Mausoleum

The Eastern Cemetery (Qarafat el Sharqiyya), as the **City of the Dead** is properly known, is the burial place of several of the greatest Mameluke sultans, among them Qaytbay, whose mausoleum, completed in 1474, is one of the finest buildings in Cairo.

The exterior of the exquisitely proportioned dome is decorated with intricate reliefs of filigree flowers upon star-shaped polygons. The tomb chamber within is of immense height, its decoration breathtakingly variegated. The City of the Dead is far from being without life. The poor have always made their homes here, while relatives visit the more recent family tombs on feast days for a picnic. *East of Sharia Salah Salem. 1km (²/3 mile) east of El Azhar Mosque, 4km (2¹/2 miles) east of Midan el Tahrir. Open: 8am–4pm. Admission charge.*

Rifai Mosque

A burial place of royalty (*see p43*). *Midan Salah el Din. 3km (1³/4 miles) southeast of Midan el Tahrir. Open: 8am–4pm. Admission charge.*

Sitt Barbara Church

This is a 7th-century Coptic church containing the relics of St Barbara, a martyr from the early days of Christianity (*see p47*). *Old Cairo (Masr el Qadima). 4.5km (2³/4 miles) south of Midan el Tahrir. Open: 8am–4pm. Free admission. Metro: Mari Girgis.*

Sultan Hassan Mosque

This is by far the finest Mameluke mosque in Cairo and regarded by many as the outstanding Islamic monument in Egypt (*see p43*). *Midan Salah el Din. 3km (1³/4 miles) southeast of Midan el Tahrir. Open: 8am–5pm. Admission charge.*

The finest Mameluke mosque in Cairo, the magnificent Sultan Hassan Mosque

MUSEUMS OF CAIRO

Museums, monuments and other ancient sites in Egypt are often closed on the spur of the moment with no warning.

Citadel museums

The **Carriage Museum** contains six royal carriages, including one of gold. The **Military Museum** is filled less with hardware than with ceremonial bric-a-brac. The **National Police Museum** includes rooms devoted to Egypt's most famous murders and assassinations, though not that of President Sadat.

Coptic Museum

This beautifully restored museum is a delight to visit. On two floors, it is dedicated to Coptic art and artifacts, with sculptures, tapestries, manuscripts, jewellery and even children's toys amongst the many treasures on display.

Amongst the museum's most famous relics are the Nag Hamadi Codices, over a thousand papyrus pages bound together as books in leather dating back to around the 4th century. Whilst walking round, don't forget to look up at the wonderfully carved wooden ceilings.
Tel: (202) 3639742. Open daily 9am–4pm. Admission charge. Metro: Mari Girgis.

Mohamed Mahmoud Khalil Museum

Mohamed Mahmoud and his wife were patrons of the arts, especially paintings, and amassed a wonderful collection of works by such celebrated artists as Gauguin, Van Gogh, Pissarro, Renoir and Sisley, to name but a few.

The sizeable collection is housed in Giza in a palace overlooking the Nile, built in the early 1920s in Art Deco and Art Nouveau French style.
1, Sharia Kafour El Akhshid, Dokki, just up the road from the Cairo Sheraton on the same side, 2km (1$^{1}/_{4}$ miles) from Midan Tahrir. Tel: (202) 3389720. Open: 10am–6pm. Closed: Mon. Admission charge.

Museum of Egyptian Antiquities

This is a unique storehouse of one of the oldest and grandest civilisations on earth. The arrangement is more or less chronological, so that starting at the entrance and walking clockwise round the ground floor, you pass from Old Kingdom through Middle Kingdom and New Kingdom exhibits (the highlight on this floor is the Akhenaton room at the rear), concluding with Ptolemaic and Roman exhibits.

The first floor contains prehistoric and early dynastic exhibits and the contents of several tombs, most notably the magnificent array of wealth from Tutankhamun's. In the Mummy Room lie the bodies of such great pharaohs as Seti I and Ramses II.
Midan el Tahrir. Tel: (202) 5754071. Open: 9am–6.30pm. Closed: Fri 11.15am–1.30pm. Admission charge, plus charge for the Mummy Room. The room housing Tutankhamun's treasures usually closes 30 minutes before the main museum. Metro: Sadat.

Islamic Art Museum

Closed for renovation. May open during 2007.

Museum of Islamic Ceramics

Built in 1924 in traditional Islamic style, and originally the home of Prince Ibrahim, this impressive palace now houses a rare collection of ceramics acquired from Islamic countries from Morocco to Iran. Egyptian pieces from various periods include vessels, jars, tiles, bowls, plates, pitchers and vases.
Corner of Sharia El Sheikh El Marsafi and Sharia Gezira, opposite the Gezira Sporting Club and just past the Cairo Marriott, 3km (1³/4 miles) from Midan Tahrir. Tel: (202) 7373298. Open: 10.30am–1.30pm, 5–9pm. Closed: Fri. Admission charge.

Agricultural Museum

Set within a beautiful garden of specimen trees, this is, in fact, three museums: the **Historical Museum** has displays of agricultural life in pharaonic times; the **Agricultural and Cotton Museum** concentrates on modern times, especially on Egypt's major cash crop; and the **Natural History and Ethnological Museum** covers the animal life, hydrology, rural crafts and culture of the Nile Valley and Delta.
At the western end of 6 October Bridge. 2km (1¹/4 miles) west of Midan el Tahrir. Tel: (202) 7614999. Open: Tue–Sun 8.30am–2.30pm. Closed: Mon. Admission charge.

Papyrus Institute

Designed to preserve the ancient Egyptian art of papyrus-making, the institute contains a museum displaying the stages in the process. Sheets of papyrus can be purchased.
On a houseboat docked at Giza's Corniche el Nil, near the Cairo Sheraton. 1.5km (1 mile) west of Midan el Tahrir. Tel: (202) 7488177. Open: 10am–7pm. Free admission.

Railway Museum

This museum has automated displays and old steam engines and carriages, plus the Khedive Ismael's private train.
Midan Ramses, next to the main railway station. 2km (1¹/4 miles) northeast of Midan el Tahrir. Tel: (202) 5763793. Open: Tue–Sun 8.30am–1pm. Closed: all day Mon. Admission charge.

Exhibits in the Museum of Egyptian Antiquities

Walk: Ibn Tulun Mosque to the Citadel

This walk takes you to four famous mosques and the Gayer-Anderson House, and concludes with a sweeping view of Cairo.

Allow 3 hours.

Begin at the Ibn Tulun Mosque.

1 Ibn Tulun Mosque

In the 9th century, when the Arab world was ruled from Baghdad, Ibn Tulun was sent to govern Egypt. He borrowed the idea for the remarkable spiral minaret (which you can climb) from the Great Mosque of Samarra in Iraq. He also introduced the technique of carved stucco which adorns the arches around the vast central court. Designed as a congregational mosque to accommodate thousands of worshippers during Friday prayers, this is the finest example of its kind in Cairo. The impression is of severe simplicity, but you should walk round the court under the arcades to appreciate the rhythm of the arches and the play that is made with light and shadow (*see p38*).

Abutting the southeast corner of the mosque is the Gayer-Anderson House.

2 Gayer-Anderson House

See p37.

Walk east along Sharia el Salibah to

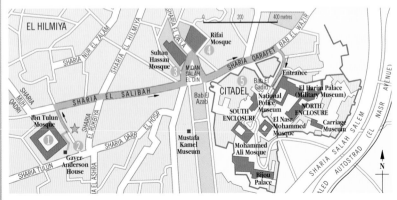

EL HILMIYA

SHARIA EL QALA

SHARIA NUR EL ZALAM

SHARIA EL HILMIYA

SHARIA MUTI

SHARIA QADRI

Ibn Tulun Mosque

SHARIA EL RUKBIYA

SHARIA EL SALIBAH

SHARIA DARB

EL HOSR

Gayer-Anderson House

SHARIA TULUN

LA EL ASHRA

Rifai Mosque

Sultan Hassan Mosque

MIDAN SALAH EL DIN

SHARIA QARAFET

BAB EL WAZIR

Entrance

El Harim Palace (Military Museum)

CITADEL

Bab El Gadid

Bab El Azab

National Police Museum

SOUTH ENCLOSURE

El Nasr Mohammed Mosque

NORTH ENCLOSURE

Carriage Museum

Mustafa Kamel Museum

Mohammed Ali Mosque

Bijou Palace

BAB EL QARAFET

SHARIA SALAH SALEM (EL NASR AVENUE)

KHALED AUTOSTRAD (EL NASR AVENUE)

200

400 metres

N

Midan Salah el Din. At its north end, two large mosques stand close together. The nearest is the Sultan Hassan Mosque.

3 Sultan Hassan Mosque

This Mameluke mosque dating from the 1350s was reputedly built of stone taken from the Pyramid of Cheops. Its huge portal with stalactite decorations (a favourite Mameluke motif) leads you into a dark corridor from which you emerge into a brilliant sun-filled central court surrounded by magnificently soaring vaults, called *liwans*.

Unlike the Ibn Tulun Mosque, designed to be a great gathering place, the Sultan Hassan was primarily a *madrasa* or theological school, the *liwans* serving as places of study. You should sit here a while, contemplating the wonderful interplay of dark and light, and how perfectly the open areas are set off by the built ones (*see p39*). Beyond the sanctuary *liwan* with its *mihrab* is Hassan's mausoleum.
Cross Sharia el Qa'la to the Rifai Mosque.

A bird's-eye view over the mosques of the city

SALADIN

Salah el Din, better known in the West as Saladin, was the chivalrous adversary of Richard the Lionheart during the Crusades. Of Kurdish stock, he became the champion of orthodox Sunni Islam, putting an end to Shi'ite Fatimid rule in Egypt and, after fortifying the Citadel, taking Jerusalem from the Crusaders in 1187.

4 Rifai Mosque

Built in the early 20th century in mock-Mameluke style, the Rifai Mosque owes its fame to the tombs of several members of Mohammed Ali's dynasty, including King Farouk (*see p39*).
Cross Midan Salah el Din to the base of the Citadel.

5 The Citadel

The western gate, Bab el Azab, is closed to the public. Here, Mohammed Ali massacred the Mamelukes in 1811, making himself absolute ruler of Egypt. Sent by the sultan in Istanbul to restore Ottoman authority after Napoleon's departure, his presence was resented by the Mamelukes. After inviting them to dinner at the Citadel, he locked the gate as they attempted to leave and shot them down with their bellies full.

Atop the Citadel (*see p36*) is the most familiar landmark in Cairo, the Mohammed Ali Mosque, famous also for its view. Looking westwards, you can trace your walk; the Rifai and Sultan Hassan mosques down below, and, further off, the great rectangle of the Ibn Tulun Mosque.

Walk: Sharia el Muizz and Khan el Khalili

This walk takes you through the heart of the medieval city, the legendary world of The Thousand and One Nights. *Much of the area is presently under restoration, but it is still an interesting walk.*

Allow 3 hours.

Begin at Bab Zuwayla.

1 Bab Zuwayla

Until the 19th century, medieval Cairo was encircled by 60 gates, of which only three remain. Eleventh-century Bab Zuwayla was the principal southern gate and the place of public executions.

Running north from the gate is Sharia el Muizz, the main street of the Fatimid city. The first building on the left is the 15th-century El Muayyad Mosque. From inside you can climb to the top of Bab Zuwayla for a fine view.
Continue north along Sharia el Muizz.

2 El Ghuri Madrasa, Mausoleum and Wakala

Just before the intersection with Sharia el Azhar are the red-and-white-striped *madrasa* (left) and mausoleum (right) of the 16th-century Mameluke sultan El Ghuri. Whirling dervishes sometimes perform at the mausoleum. At the intersection turn right. After 100m (110yds) is El Ghuri's *wakala*, the best-preserved example of a merchants' hostel in Cairo (*see p37*).
Retrace your steps, cross Sharia el Azhar and continue north along Sharia el Muizz.

3 Khan el Khalili

The Spice Bazaar is on the edge of the vast warren that is Khan el Khalili (*see p38*). Turning right at the market street of Muski you come to the Perfume Bazaar. Sharia el Muski continues east into a large square overlooked to the south by the 10th-century El Azhar Mosque (*see p34*), and to the north by Sayyidna el Hussein Mosque (non-Muslims not normally admitted).

To the west of the square is Fishawi's, a famous café where you can pause for refreshments (*see p169*).
From Sharia el Muski, walk 200m (220yds) north along Sharia el Muizz.

4 Qalaun Madrasa and Mausoleum

On your left you see three domes, each with a stout minaret – a splendid cluster of religious buildings by the Mameluke sultans Qalaun, El Nasr and Barquq. The finest of these complexes is the late 13th-century work of Qalaun. Inside, on the left, is the *madrasa* or theological school; on the right is Qalaun's mausoleum, a masterpiece of Mameluke architecture, richly ornamented with mother-of-pearl mosaics beneath a soaring dome pierced by colourful stained-glass windows.

Walk north along Sharia el Muizz, then turn right into Haret el Darb el Asfar.

5 Bayt el Suhaymi

See p36.
Continue north along Lidin Allah.

6 El Hakim Mosque

The 11th-century Fatimid Caliph el Hakim declared himself God and countered objections by chopping off heads and burning down half of Cairo. He was assassinated at the instigation of his sister.

For centuries, an aura of dread hung about the mosque, and it was allowed to crumble. It has now been restored and looks much brighter.

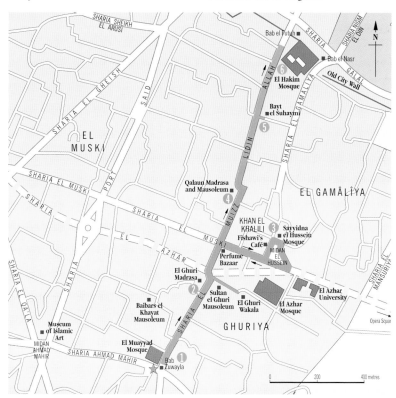

Walk: Coptic Cairo

This walk introduces you to some of the oldest churches in Egypt, as well as to its oldest synagogue.

Allow 1 hour.

Begin at the Mari Girgis metro station, facing the towers of the Roman fortress.

1 Roman Fortress

The section of wall and two towers are part of a Roman fortress which was built around 30 BC, after Augustus had defeated Antony and Cleopatra. The fortress once encompassed all the sites covered in this walk, but much of it was demolished by the British in the 19th century, leaving only these ruins.

After purchasing a ticket to the Coptic Museum and passing across its inner courtyard, you can descend to the level of the Roman water gate, into which the Nile still seeps, and step along raised walkways beneath arches and vaults. Above you is El Muallaqa Church.

2 Coptic Museum

The two Roman towers of the fortress also mark the entrance to the grounds of the Coptic Museum (*see p40*), its exhibits gathered from ancient churches and houses.

Leave between the Roman towers and turn left, following the walls round to the steps rising to the level of El Muallaqa.

3 El Muallaqa Church (Church of The Virgin)

This is known as the Hanging Church because it lies on beams laid across the two bastions of the Roman water gate. It was probably built after the 7th-century Arab conquest, once the walls had become redundant. The interior is intricately decorated with pointed arches, cedar panelling and translucent ivory screens. The carved marble pulpit is the finest in Egypt. On the right-hand wall is a 10th-century icon of the Virgin and Child, and an icon of St Mark, by tradition the founder of Christianity in Egypt (*see p38*).

Return to Sharia Mari Girgis, turn right, and follow the walls, passing the two Roman towers until you come to a small stairway which leads you to a passage through the walls. At the end of the street, turn right.

Walk: Coptic Cairo

4 Abu Sarga Church (Church of St Sargius)

The Church of Abu Sarga, thought to date from the 5th century, is one of the oldest surviving churches in Egypt. According to tradition, the Holy Family found refuge in the crypt (once a cave), after their flight from Herod. Faded paintings of the Apostles, probably 8th-century, adorn the columns of the nave, while 12th-century carved wooden panels on the altar screen depict the scenes of the Nativity and Last Supper (*see p34*).
Turn right out of Abu Sarga and then left at the corner. At the end of the street you see Sitt Barbara to the right.

5 Sitt Barbara Church (Church of St Barbara)

Built in the 7th century, its lofty wooden roof probably dates to Fatimid times. The relics of St Barbara are in the right-hand sanctuary. She had the misfortune, so legend goes, to be born in the 3rd century to a pagan father who, on discovering that she was a Christian, turned her over to the Roman authorities to be tortured and beheaded (*see p39*).
Turn left out of the church to the gateway crowned with the Star of David.

6 Ben Ezra Synagogue

This is the oldest synagogue in Egypt, restored in the 12th century by the Rabbi of Jerusalem, Abraham Ben Ezra, though probably converted from a church in the 9th century. A far older tradition claims that Jeremiah came here to preach after Nebuchadnezzar had destroyed Jerusalem in the 6th century BC (*see p36*).

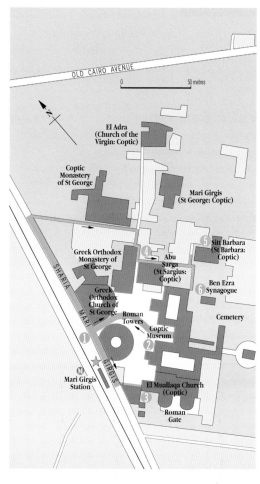

Cairo environs

Around 3100 BC, Upper and Lower Egypt were united under the rule of Menes, who established the First Dynasty and founded Memphis as his capital. The palaces, shrines and houses were made of mud brick but at its necropolis of Saqqâra, the tombs of the dead were built of stone to endure eternity. Saqqâra was the world's first 'city' of stone. Some of its tombs resembled the single-storey houses of the living at Memphis, while the pharaoh Zoser had a grander idea. By placing a succession of ever smaller tombs one on top of the other, he created his Step Pyramid. Subsequently, over 80 pyramids were constructed, of which the Great Pyramids at Gîza are the largest and most famous.

GÎZA PYRAMIDS COMPLEX

The long straight road west from Cairo passes through the built-up suburb of Gîza and finally curves sharply to the left and mounts the desert plateau (11km/7 miles). Alternatively, take the ring road, following signs for the Pyramids. Once at the site, before you is the Pyramid of Cheops, the oldest and largest of the three Gîza Pyramids. Beyond stand the pyramids of Chephren and Mycerinus, in descending order of age and size along a southwest axis, each identically oriented 8.5 degrees west of magnetic north. Built between 2600 BC and 2525 BC, they were probably aligned precisely with the North Star.

Near the edge of the desert, and accessible by boat during the inundation, was a modest valley chapel. From here a walled-in causeway led up to the

Pyramid of Cheops

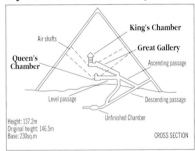

King's Chamber
Air shafts
Great Gallery
Queen's Chamber
Ascending passage
Level passage
Descending passage
Unfinished Chamber
Height: 137.2m
Original height: 146.5m
Base: 230sq.m
CROSS SECTION

funerary temple on the east side of the pyramid, where the soul of the dead pharaoh could emerge from its tomb to partake of the offered feasts. Not all of these structures have survived. On the sides of the Pyramid of Cheops, wooden solar boats have been found in pits (*see p50*), and there are smaller pyramids, some for royal wives, as well as rows of flat-topped tombs called *mastabas* for nobles and royal princes.

Open: daily 7am–4pm; site open until 8pm in winter, midnight in summer. Admission charge. Solar Boat Museum. Open: daily 7am–3.30pm. Admission charge.

Pyramid of Cheops

Once, all the pyramids had smooth sides of polished stone, but the casing on the Pyramid of Cheops has entirely gone, and you see instead the underlying tiered courses of 2,500,000 limestone blocks. Inside, a descending corridor reaches a chamber in the bedrock, left unfinished, possibly because of flooding, while a detour off the ascending corridor leads to the so-called Queen's Chamber. Far grander is the ascending Great Gallery, which leads to the King's Chamber. On the north and south walls of this, 1m (40in) above the floor, you can see the ventilation shafts which reach to the surface of the pyramid. The weight of 95m (310ft) of pyramid sits above your head, but the pressure is redirected away from the burial chamber by five successive relieving chambers above the granite roofing slabs. Cheops' name was found inscribed in the relieving chambers; otherwise, the King's Chamber contains neither inscriptions nor decorations, and its sarcophagus was found empty.

The Great Pyramid of Cheops

Cheops' funerary solar boat found in perfect condition displays intricate craftsmanship

Pyramid of Chephren

Chephren's Pyramid is almost as large as Cheops', and seems larger as it stands on higher ground. The impression of greater height is also due to the casing stones which are intact towards the top. Its interior, however, is less interesting. Its tomb chamber also contained an empty sarcophagus. All three pyramids seemed sealed when entered during the 19th century. In fact, each had been looted at some ancient time.

Pyramid of Mycerinus

At 66.5m (218ft) in height, this is the smallest of the three main pyramids. A 9th-century caliph attempted to demolish the pyramids altogether, starting with that of Mycerinus. Eight months and 170,000 blocks of stone later, he gave up, leaving the gouge you see on the north face.

Solar Boat Museum

Some say that solar boats were built to ferry the pharaoh as he followed the sun god across the skies. Five solar boat pits have been found round the base of the Pyramid of Cheops. The first three were empty, but in 1954 and 1987, two dismantled but perfectly preserved boats of Syrian cedar were discovered. The latter has been left within its pit, but the former, 4,600 years old and 43m (47yds) long, has been reassembled and put on display in the specially built museum at the south face of the Pyramid of Cheops.

Sound and Light

The Sphinx plays the dramatic role of narrator in this booming and atmospheric programme telling the story of the Pyramids. Bring a sweater; even in summer the evenings can get cool.

The Sphinx

A limestone outcrop was left standing in the quarry from which many of the blocks for Cheops' Pyramid were cut. His son Chephren had the idea of shaping it into a figure with a lion's body and a god's face – although perhaps the face is Chephren's own. The Turks used the Sphinx for target practice in the 16th century and shot off its nose. The beard is at the British Museum. Though 20m (66ft) high and 48.5m (159ft) long, the Sphinx may not seem as large as you might imagine, as much of its bulk crouches within the quarry. The poor quality of its stone has contributed to its erosion.

Valley Temple of Chephren
By the south flank of the Sphinx, Chephren's valley temple has been well preserved by its long burial under the sands. Majestically assembled from pink Aswân granite, its square monolithic pillars support massive architraves. Some authorities think Chephren's mummification took place here; it is more generally agreed that this is where the 'Opening of the

Mouth' ceremony took place, the *ka* or soul of the pharaoh entering and leaving his body.

SOUND AND LIGHT
The Sound and Light pavilion faces the Sphinx and is signposted left off the main road to the Pyramids, 1km (²/3 mile) before the Mena House Oberoi, 10km (6 miles) west of Cairo's Midan el Tahrir (*tel: (202) 3852880*). There are two evening performances – 6.30pm and 7.30pm (times differ according to season), as follows: Mon: English and French; Tue: English and Italian; Wed: English and French; Thur: Arabic and English; Fri: English and French; Sat: English and Spanish; Sun: French and German. Admission charge.

Pyramids of Gîza

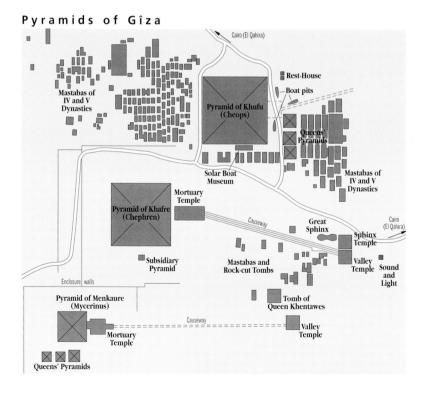

MEMPHIS

Most probably beginning as a fortress from which Menes controlled the land and water routes between Upper and Lower Egypt, Memphis was the capital of the country throughout the Old Kingdom period. Though New Kingdom Egypt was ruled from Thebes, the former capital remained a great city until overtaken by Ptolemaic Alexandria. Centuries of Nile mud have since swallowed Memphis, and there is now little to see.

Colossus of Ramses II

The New Kingdom pharaoh Ramses II was one of those who continued to embellish Memphis with great buildings and statues, including a pair of colossal statues of himself which probably stood outside the Temple of Ptah.

The impressive statue of Ramses II

MEMPHIS

The ruins of Memphis are at the village of Mit Rahina, 3km (1³/₄ miles) from El Badrashein, on the west bank of the Nile, south of Cairo. Memphis is 32km (20 miles) south of Cairo by road, 21km (13 miles) south of the Giza Pyramids, and 6km (3³/₄ miles) southeast of Saqqâra. It is included in most tours to Saqqâra; otherwise the only practical way of getting here is by hiring a taxi. Open: daily 8am–5pm (4pm in winter). Admission charge.

Hauled out of the mud in 1820, one used to stand outside the main Cairo railway station but was moved to a new site in 2006. The other was offered to the British Museum – which failed to collect it. So here it lies, flat on its back, specially encased within a modern building. Other smaller statues stand or lie about in the surrounding gardens, including a large alabaster sphinx from the New Kingdom period.

Mummification beds

Across the road from the garden with its sphinx are the alabaster mummification beds where the bodies of the Apis bulls were soaked in a liquid containing natron (a natural salt) to dehydrate them in preparation for burial (*see* Serapeum, *pp54–5*).

Temple of Ptah

The remains of this temple to the venerated god of Memphis can be seen only faintly. They lie waterlogged near the mummification beds.

SAQQÂRA

The sands wash about your feet nearly everywhere at Saqqâra which has more of a desert feel about it than Gîza. Named after Sokkar, the Memphite god of the dead, this was a necropolis for over 3,000 years, though most of its greatest monuments belong to the Old Kingdom. It was here that the ancient Egyptians first put into practice on a grand scale their attempt to defeat time – by replacing the perishable mud brick of their homes and shrines at Memphis with eternal replicas in stone.

Imhotep Museum

This museum, near the ticket office, was opened in 2006 and contains a fascinating cross section of objects including a stone sphinx, contents of a tomb dating back to between the 11th and 12th Dynasties and a beautifully preserved mummy of King Merenrai. There is a small room dedicated to Jean Philippe Lauer, a Frenchman who spent over 70 years restoring monuments here.

Mastaba of Akhti-Hotep and Ptah-Hotep

Belonging to the priest Ptah-Hotep and his father, the vizier Akhti-Hotep, this 5th-Dynasty double *mastaba* is outstanding for the variety and quality of its coloured reliefs. The entrance corridor has reliefs in progress. The preliminary drawings are in red, and the master's corrections in black. Across a pillared hall you enter Ptah-Hotep's

SAQQÂRA

Saqqâra is on the desert plateau above Memphis, 30km (18¹/₂ miles) south of Cairo by road, 19km (12 miles) south of the Gîza Pyramids, and 6km (3³/₄ miles) north-west from Memphis. The only practical ways of getting here are by guided tour or taxi, or by horse or camel across the desert from the Gîza Pyramids (*see p48*). Open: daily 8am–5pm (4pm in winter). Admission charge.

tomb chamber. A relief on the right wall shows Ptah-Hotep in the panther-skin of a high priest, seated at a cornucopian offering table, a goblet raised to his lips. A catalogue of daily events fills the left wall, including boys and girls playing games and a cow giving birth. The details are vivid; notice, for example, the hare emerging from its hole with a cricket in its mouth. Above the entrance you see Ptah-Hotep preparing for the day. A manicurist works at his hands, a pedicurist at his feet, musicians are entertaining him, with dogs and a pet monkey nearby. Across the pillared hall is the similar, but less finely decorated, tomb chamber of Akhti-Hotep.

The 18th-century BC alabaster sphinx at Memphis, surrounded by palm-lined pathways

Mastaba of Mereruka

Mereruka was vizier to a 6th-Dynasty pharaoh, and his 32-room *mastaba* is the largest at Saqqâra. The entry passage shows him painting a picture of the seasons and playing a board game to pass away eternity, while the first three chambers are decorated with scenes of hunting, furniture-making and goldsmiths at work. At the far end of the *mastaba*, in a chapel with six pillars, is a statue of Mereruka himself. The scenes to the left of this show the domestication of gazelles, goats and hyenas.

Mastaba of Ti

Ti was overseer of royal farms and mortuary temples in the 5th Dynasty. He was also the royal hairdresser.

The reliefs in Ti's beautifully decorated funerary chamber rival those of Ptah-Hotep's, and exceed them in

Saqqâra

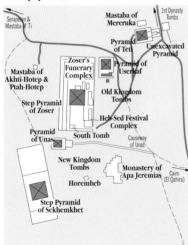

variety. The highlight here is a relief of Ti sailing through the marshes. The scene is full of symbolism, for this is Ti fighting against the forces of evil as represented by the hunted hippo, and of chaos represented by the fish and birds. The crocodile, at once being bitten by and biting the hippopotamus, was sacred and represents good.

Through a slot in the far wall, in the *serdab* (closed corridor with statues of the dead), you can see a statue of Ti. Here his soul or *ka* awaited the offerings brought to the chamber. You will notice that his hair, or wig, is well done.

Pyramid of Unas

Unas was the last pharaoh of the 5th Dynasty, and the 350 years from the Step Pyramid through the Great Pyramids at Gîza to this heap of rubble mark the rise and fall of the Old Kingdom sun cult. Unfortunately, its core was shoddily built of loose stone and rubble; the pyramid is not safe to enter. The tomb chamber is entirely covered with inscriptions celebrating eternal life and the newly popular resurrection cult of Osiris. *May be closed.*

The Serapeum

The Serapeum, where the Apis bulls were buried, is the strangest place at Saqqâra. Long, gloomily lit, rock-cut galleries beneath the desert are lined with gigantic vaults, each vault containing a bull-sized black sarcophagus. For generations, these

Apis bulls were buried like kings, for they were believed to be incarnations of Ptah, the god of Memphis. The oldest galleries date back to Ramses II, although those sometimes open to the public belong to the period of the Ptolemies. (*See* Mummification beds, *p52.*) *Currently closed.*

Step Pyramid of Zoser

The Step Pyramid is the central piece of an extensive funerary complex built for the 3rd-Dynasty pharaoh Zoser, who lived around 2700 BC. Surrounded by an enclosure wall probably built in imitation of the city walls of Memphis, this first pyramid, 62m (203ft) high, was created by placing a series of ever smaller *mastabas* one on top of the other.

The Great South Court, with its frieze of cobras, and the shrines in the Heb-Sed Court next to it, represent the ritual Heb-Sed race run in Memphis by the pharaoh during his 30th jubilee celebrations, impressing and reinvigorating a united Upper and Lower Egypt with his spiritual strength.

There is a relief of Zoser running the Heb-Sed race in the South Tomb, which is decorated with blue faïence tiles. It is reached via a deep shaft.

Passing along the east side of the Step Pyramid you come to the House of the South, its lotus capitals symbolising Upper Egypt, and the House of the North, with papyrus capitals on its graceful columns to symbolise Lower Egypt. Against the north side of the pyramid is the *serdab*, in which stands a *ka* statue of Zoser. His eyes are forever fixed on the North Star, the star that never sets and so never dies.

Part of the extensive Sed Festival complex at Zoser's Step Pyramid

Desert ride: Gîza to Saqqâra

This journey across the desert and along the edge of the cultivated zone can be done by either horse or camel. It allows you to see several rarely visited pyramids and sun temples along the way. A camel will cost more to hire than a horse. Most people, however, will find a horse more comfortable over this distance. Outside summer bring something warm to wear; the desert can get very windy and chilly.

Allow 3 hours in each direction, plus time to look around Saqqâra. Or, ride to Saqqâra and return to Gîza by taxi.

Start from the stables behind the Sound and Light pavilion, which is the best place to hire your mount.

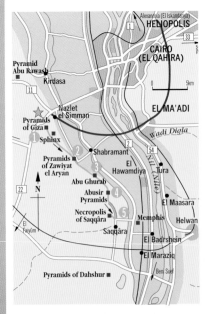

1 Pyramids of Gîza

You pass a modern Muslim cemetery on your left and then head south across the sands. To the east you will see the cultivated zone of the Nile Valley. The encroaching outskirts of Cairo soon disappear from sight and behind you there is a wonderful view of the Gîza Pyramids (*see pp48–51*), which belong to the 3rd-Dynasty period, standing alone on the desert plateau.

After about an hour and a quarter you come to two pyramids.

2 Pyramids of Zawiyat el Aryan

The northerly Unfinished Pyramid, abandoned during the 4th Dynasty some time after the Gîza Pyramids, is surrounded by unused granite and limestone blocks. Fifteen minutes to the southeast, and nearer the cultivation, is the **Layer Pyramid**, older than those at Gîza though it belongs to the 3rd Dynasty. Built of small blocks, it was perhaps meant to be a step pyramid.

About half an hour south, near the cultivation (where roses are the local speciality), are two sun temples.

3 Abu Ghurab Sun Temples

The sun was always venerated by the ancient Egyptians. It is said that pyramids and obelisks, with a pyramid-shape at the top and sometimes covered with gold and silver, imitated the sun's rays spreading across the earth. In the courtyard of the northerly 5th-Dynasty **Sun Temple of Nyuserre** stand an altar and the base of a solar obelisk. The obelisk has vanished, but you can climb up within the base for views across the desert.

Immediately to the southeast, passing by the Sun Temple of Userkaf, are the pyramids of Abusir.

4 Abusir Pyramids

The northernmost **Pyramid of Sahure** is badly damaged, though you can crawl through a narrow passage into its tomb chamber and also climb to the summit. From here there is a fine panorama of the other 5th-Dynasty pyramids in this cluster and their attendant mortuary temples. The group is named after the nearby village.

Continuing on, you pass the pyramids of **Nyuserre**, **Neferikare** and **Neferefre**. Neither the first nor last of these was ever finished owing to the early deaths of their pharaohs.

Neferikare also died early, but work continued, although what had begun with red granite and limestone was completed in mud brick.

Abusir is not always open to the public. Hours are 8am–4pm. Admission charge.

5 Approaching Saqqâra

You can now clearly see the Step Pyramid and other structures at Saqqâra (*see pp53–5*), no more than half an hour's ride south, and beyond that the **Red Pyramid** and the **Bent Pyramid** at Dahshur, both built by a 4th-Dynasty pharaoh, together with another pyramid now collapsed.

Dahshur is usually open: 8am–4pm. Admission charge.

Both the camel and its owner proudly solicit your custom

Excursions from Cairo

Whatever your interest in its ancient sites, there is fascination in a drive or train ride through the green and watery landscape of the Nile Delta, the river's last great outpouring before it reaches the Mediterranean Sea.

THE DELTA

The Nile Delta area is extraordinarily flat, and so the sky is vast. The sails of feluccas billow on the river amid fields furrowed by canals. Buffalo turn wheels for grinding or pumping, and brightly coloured figures move through an abundance of cotton, rice and maize.

In antiquity the Nile had seven arms here. Now it has only two. One flows into the Mediterranean Sea at Dumyât (Damietta), the other flows out at Rashid (Rosetta). As all the other tributaries dried up or changed course, cities were abandoned, often then disappearing beneath the mud. In Upper Egypt, where the river has been confined to its narrow valley, much of the past has been preserved. In the Delta, history has far too often been erased.

Yet the Delta knew greatness. From their capital in the Eastern Delta, the Hyksos, a foreign people of uncertain origin, ruled over the whole of Egypt during the 2nd Intermediate Period, and in the Eastern Delta, too, was the Land of Goshen which was mentioned in *Genesis* and *Exodus*.

The dynasty of Seti I had its roots in the Delta, and his son, Ramses II, built his northern capital, Pi-Ramses, here. Throughout the first millennium BC the Delta dominated the affairs of Egypt – various dynasties had their capitals at Tanis, Bubastis and Sais. The Delta's importance became all the greater when the Ptolemies built their capital at Alexandria.

VISITING

Like the arms of the Nile itself, the principal roads and railway lines fan out northwards from Cairo, while links between the Eastern and Western Delta are poor. The Western Delta can be visited en route to Alexandria, which is linked to Cairo by the main railway line and the Agricultural Road, while **Rashid** (Rosetta – *see p75*) should be visited from Alexandria itself. Sites in the Eastern Delta are best visited by making a loop around Zagazig, while Dumyât would be a separate excursion.

Bubastis

Near Zagazig, Bubastis is one of the most ancient sites in Egypt. The name means House of the Goddess Bastet, who was represented as a lioness, and later as a graceful cat. The ruins of her temple, founded during the Old Kingdom but rebuilt during the 22nd Dynasty, can be seen here. Beneath it are galleries for the burial of cats.
3km (2 miles) south of Zagazig, along the road to Bilbeis. Open: daily 9am–4pm. Free admission. Service taxis (which will drop you off at Bubastis), buses and trains all run the 80km (50 miles) from Cairo to Zagazig.

Dumyât (Damietta)

Situated 15km (9 miles) from the Mediterranean on a narrow strip of land between the eastern arm of the Nile and Lake Manzala, Dumyât is a thriving port and industrial centre, preserving numerous mansions from the Ottoman period. Birdwatchers are attracted to the lake, which is, in fact, a brackish lagoon that extends eastwards towards Port Said.

Famous at the time of the Crusades as Damietta, St Louis of France landed here in 1249, but was captured and ransomed. During an earlier attack on the city in 1218, St Francis of Assisi courageously crossed enemy lines and offered to enter a fiery furnace on the condition that should he come out alive, the sultan and his people would convert to Christianity. The sultan replied by giving the saint a lesson in humanity and common sense, saying that gambling with one's life was not a valid proof of one's God.
210km (130 miles) northeast of Cairo and served by train and bus.

Drying and cleaning corn prior to packaging

Pi-Ramses

Mentioned in *Exodus 1:11* and *12:37* as the city built for the pharaoh by the afflicted children of Israel, and as their point of departure out of Egypt under Moses' leadership, the site of Pi-Ramses is thought to be marked by the negligible ruins found at Qantir.
Qantir, near Faqus. 45km (28 miles) northeast of Zagazig.

Sais

Though at times the capital during the Late Dynastic Period, there is nothing to see today at Sais. The site has suffered from the activities of the *sebakhin*, and is an interesting example of how Egypt lives upon its past. In a land where wood is a rarity

and animal dung has long been used for fuel, the *fellahin* have turned to the debris mounds or *koms* of ancient towns. These yield a rich soil called *sebakh* which is used as a fertiliser. The once royal city of Sais is now a waterlogged depression.
30km (18 1/2 miles) to the northwest of Tanta.

Tanis

Egyptologists once argued that Tanis was the site of Pi-Ramses. Though this impressive lineage is now disputed, the fact that these are the most impressive ruins in the Delta region cannot be denied.

The **Temple of Amun** is spectacular for its fallen colossal statuary, and you can enter the royal tombs of its 21st- and 22nd-Dynasty pharaohs, whose capital this was. The splendid gold

A Bedouin from Siwa Oasis

masks, inlaid jewellery and silver sarcophagus discovered here in 1939, which rival the treasures of Tutankhamun, are now in the Egyptian Antiquities Museum in Cairo (*see p40*). A sacred lake and the remains of two other temples are evident within the enclosure walls.

Near San el Hagar. 74km (46 miles) northeast of Zagazig. Some tours come here, otherwise take a taxi and have it wait for you. Open: daily 9am–4pm. Admission charge.

Tanta

This nondescript city, with a population of over 350,000, is Egypt's fifth largest. It jumps to life at the end of the October cotton harvest, when as many as two million people, from all around the Arab world, attend the joyous *moulid* centred round the mosque and tomb of a 13th-century Sufi saint, Said Ahmed el Badawi (*see feature opposite*).

90km (56 miles) northwest of Cairo, on the railway line to Alexandria.

Zagazig

Dating only from the 1820s, this is the birthplace of Ahmed Orabi, leader of the 1882 revolt against British influence. Zagazig is a good place to begin a tour of the Eastern Delta. Its Orabi Museum contains objects from nearby Bubastis.

85km (53 miles) northeast of Cairo from where it is well served by various types of transport: taxi, bus and train. Orabi Museum open: 9am–1pm. Closed: Tue.

The ruins at Tanis

The Faiyûm and the Western Desert

Although almost entirely surrounded by the Western Desert, the Faiyûm is not a true oasis because it depends on the Nile. Failure to maintain the Faiyûm's irrigation system during the late Roman period caused Lake Qarun to shrink, leaving ghost towns all round its desert perimeter (see pp64–5).

THE FAIYÛM

Revival began under the British, and the Faiyûm now possesses 2,300km (1,429 miles) of capillary canals – equal to the entire length of the Nile through Egypt. Cereals, fruit and flowers grow again in wonderful profusion, and increasing numbers of visitors are attracted to the Faiyûm as much for its rural charm as for its ancient sites.

Kom Aushim (Ancient Karanis)

Offering a good panorama of the lake and oasis from the rim of the Faiyûm depression, Karanis is the most accessible of the abandoned Ptolemaic towns. Beyond the roadside museum are ancient streets and houses, and two temples dedicated to crocodile gods.

Served by buses and service taxis plying the desert road between Cairo (76km/ 47 miles) and Medinet el Faiyûm (30km/ 18 1/2 miles). Museum open: 9am–4pm. Closed: Mon. Admission charge.

Medinet el Faiyûm

All roads and canals radiate from this ordinary market centre, site of the Ptolemaic city of Crocodilopolis.

Obelisk of Sesostris I

This 12th-Dynasty obelisk stands at a roundabout as you arrive from Cairo.

Qaytbay Mosque

This Mameluke mosque (AD 1476), which has columns from ancient Crocodilopolis, is a 10-minute walk west from the tourist office at the centre of town.

Souk

Near the Qaytbay Mosque is a warren of market streets selling food, spices,

---

THE FAIYÛM

The Faiyûm, with its ancient sites and souk (above), is reached by bus or service taxi to Medinet el Faiyûm, 100km (62 miles) from Cairo. You might need a police escort (see p178).

copperware, jewellery and a variety of bric-a-brac.

Waterwheels

Four waterwheels groan away outside the Cafeteria el Medina by the tourist office at the centre of town. There are 200 of these throughout the oasis. In 30 minutes you can walk to the Seven Waterwheels, a Faiyûm landmark, north of town.

OASES OF THE WESTERN DESERT
Baharîya

White-walled houses and a 6th-century Coptic church mark the old quarter of **Bawiti** on a ridge, Qarat el-Farargi, overlooking palm groves. One kilometre (²/₃ mile) west is the sister village of **El Qasr**, its houses incorporating stones from a 26th-Dynasty temple and a Roman arch. A recent discovery is the Mummies Valley, which is not open to the public. Four mummies can, however, be seen at the local museum. *Open 9am–4pm. Free admission.*

Dakhla

Dakhla is the most beautiful of the oases. Its two main towns are **Mut**, with hot springs nearby at **Mut Talata**, and, 27km (17 miles) to the west, **El Qasr**, the original fortified settlement of the oasis which has a Mameluke mosque and a Roman temple close by.

Farafra

Isolated Farafra has a picturesque old quarter and walled palm groves for delightful walks. The atmosphere is religiously conservative.

El Khârga

El Khârga town is a developed and unromantic place, although at ancient **Hibis**, on its northern outskirts, there is a Temple of Amun, and 1km (²/₃ mile) beyond, at **Baqawat**, there is an early Christian necropolis.

Siwa

The well-preserved Temple of Amun rises from vast groves of date palms and fruit trees. Here, Alexander came to consult the oracle and was told he was a god. Siwa continues to deliver romance, and, although its crumbling fortified village has been abandoned for newer houses, traditions remain strong. Veiled women drape themselves in silver jewellery, Berber is spoken instead of Arabic, and local festivals and marriage customs are still observed – though the ancient custom of homosexual marriage was discontinued in the mid-20th century.

OASES OF THE WESTERN DESERT

With the exception of Siwa near the Libyan border, which is reached by travelling west from Alexandria to Mersa Matruh and then south, the oases of the Western Desert are linked by a 1,000km (621-mile) road looping out from Cairo and back to the Nile at Asyût. All can be reached by bus and service taxi. It is possible you may have to have a police escort (*see p178*). There are flights to Khârga.

Tour: The Faiyûm

When in late Roman times the irrigation system of the Faiyûm began to fail through neglect, a number of Ptolemaic towns and more ancient sites around the periphery of the oasis were abandoned to the advancing sands. Medinet el Faiyûm is the transport hub from which to start each visit. The tourist office at the centre of town, by the café with the four waterwheels, can give you information on different means of touring this area.

Allow 1 day if you have a car. By public transport, select one or two sights to visit. Be prepared to have a police escort whether travelling privately or by public transport.

The direct route to Lake Qarun is via Sanhur. From here, you can approach the Auberge du Lac from the east or by way of the lakeside village of Shakshuk.

1 Auberge du Lac

The Auberge du Lac was originally King Farouk's hunting lodge, but is now a hotel, crowded on weekends. From its veranda you can look out over the lake, which attracts great numbers of migratory birds, including the pink flamingo and thousands of ducks. *From here or Shakshuk you can hire a boatman for an hour's journey across the lake to Dimeh el Siba.*

2 Dimeh el Siba

In Ptolemaic times this was a lakeside town called Soknopaiou Nesos. Now you must walk up a rather steep 3km

(1 3/4-mile) track from the north shore of the lake to reach this scene of majestic desolation.

A 400m (440yd) processional way begins at what was the lakeshore and passes through the town gate to the **Temple of Soknopaiou and Isis** with several reliefs, one of Ptolemy II praying before Amun.

The settlement was a fortified caravan station from where the long journey across the desert to distant oases began.

There are service taxis from the Auberge du Lac, Shakshuk and Medinet el Faiyûm to Ibshaway, then on to the village of Qasr Qarun near the western extremity of the lake.

3 Qasr Qarun

Beside the village are the remains of the Ptolemaic settlement of **Dionysias**, its most notable feature a sandstone Ptolemaic temple dedicated to the crocodile god Sobek. You can explore its labyrinthine interior, and climb up to the roof for distant views over the oasis and desert.

To reach ancient Narmouthis, known as Medinet Madi, take a bus to Menshat Sef, a village south of Abu Gandir. Walking west from here, follow the canal, cross over the first bridge and take the narrow track south. Within an hour you will see a stone hut on

the desert's rise. Just beyond it is Medinet Madi.

4 Medinet Madi

A processional way lined by lions and sphinxes approaches the 12th-Dynasty temple dedicated to Sobek which is covered with numerous reliefs. The mud-brick remains of the town lie about, while an embankment to the north of the temple was in fact the storm beach of Lake Qarun.

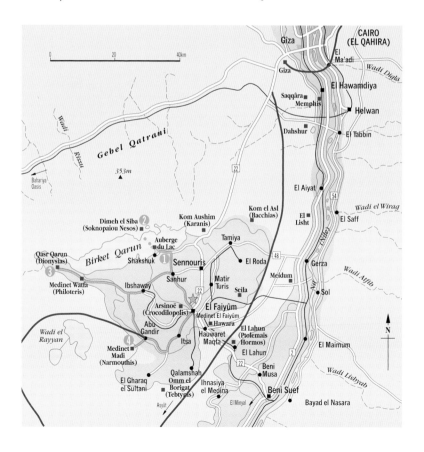

Wadi Natrûn

The Coptic monasteries of the Wadi Natrûn, once isolated in the Western Desert, now lie within sight of the 200km (125-mile) Desert Road built between Cairo and Alexandria in the 1930s. Founded early in the 4th century, they are among the oldest monasteries in the world. They look like fortresses, their great walls surrounding a central keep built in defence against Bedouin raids. Often rebuilt both within and without, nothing stands from before the period of the 7th century. Today, these and other desert monasteries are at the heart of the spiritual revival of the Coptic Church, and their monks are recruited from the universities and the professions.

Monastery of St Baramus (Deir el Baramus)

Parts of the Church of el Adra (the Virgin) in this monastery date from the 9th century, and alongside is the old refectory. From the 11m- (36ft-) high walls you can look down into the monastery's arbour-shaded courtyard, and out into the surrounding desert where hermits' caves can be seen.

Monastery of St Bishoi (Deir Anba Bishoi)

From his tomb in the 9th-century Church of St Bishoi, the saint himself is said occasionally to reach out and shake the hands of believers. The atmosphere suggested by the tale, however, has been stripped away by much modern rebuilding, making this the least interesting of the four monasteries.

GETTING TO THE MONASTERIES

From the Rest House, 95km (60 miles) northwest of Cairo on the Desert Road to Alexandria, a road runs 3km (1^3/$_4$ miles) to Bir Hooker village. There the road forks, right 12km (7^1/$_2$ miles) for the Monastery of Baramus, left 7km (4^1/$_4$ miles) for the monasteries of the Syrians and St Bishoi.

The Monastery of St Makarius is most easily reached from the Desert Road: 82km (51 miles) north of Cairo, a road runs west for 8km (5 miles) to the monastery. Buses and service taxis running between Cairo and Alexandria stop at the Rest House, where you can hire a local taxi. Alternatively, hire a taxi from Cairo for the day.

All four monasteries are generally open daily from 9am to 5pm, but some or all may be fully or partly closed during periods of fasting. Visitors to the Monastery of St Makarius need a letter of introduction from the Coptic Patriarch in Cairo. (*See p178 for details on visiting and staying overnight.*)

Monastery of St Makarius (Deir Abu Maqar)

You might almost think this a holiday village for monks when you enter the monastery courtyard surrounded by new cells, a refectory, library, guesthouse, bakery and other amenities. Much of ancient interest still survives.

In the large Church of St Makarius, the 7th-century domed sanctuary of John the Baptist is decorated with a winged cherub and the four horses of the Apocalypse. On the arch before the sanctuary are finely painted 11th-century scenes of Christ's burial. The three-storey keep, entered by a drawbridge, is also 11th-century. There are four churches within it, with wonderful paintings on their walls.

Monastery of the Syrians (Deir el Suryani)

With a huge hull supporting a super-structure of domes, towers and crosses, this most fascinating of the four monasteries is like a great ship riding the waves of desert sand.

The 10th-century Church of el Adra (the Virgin) in the complex is remarkable for the decorative doors facing the sanctuary, and more so for the beautiful frescos in the semidomes of the choir.

On the right are the Annunciation and Nativity; on the left, the Dormition of the Virgin. At the opposite end of the church is a grotto, said to have been the hermit's cell of St Bishoi, built long before the church.

Wadi Natrûn

Fresco of the Annunciation in the Church of el Adra, Monastery of the Syrians

Alexandria

Alexandria is Egypt's major port and the country's second-largest city, with a population of over 5¹/₂ million. Unlike the rest of the country, it is cool and wet in winter, with refreshing Mediterranean breezes in summer. Alexander the Great founded the city in 332 BC on the site of a small fishing village, Rhakotis. He built a causeway connecting the island of Pharos (where Ras el Tin Palace and Qaytbay Fort stand) to the mainland, creating two great harbours, which became the basis of Alexandria's prosperity.

This spirit of invention was continued under Alexander's Greek successors, the Ptolemies, who built the famous Pharos lighthouse, established the Great Library, and founded the Mouseion, a research institute where remarkable advances were made in mathematics, engineering and medicine. Later still, Alexandria played a formative role in

the development of Christian thought, adding Greek philosophy to Jewish and Egyptian beliefs.

Little of this ancient and illustrious city survives, however. After the 7th-century Arab invasion, Alexandria declined. Refounded early in the 19th century by Mohammed Ali, foreigners were attracted by the promise of

Alexandria

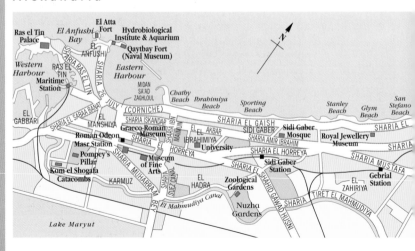

trading opportunities, especially in cotton. Cosmopolitan and lively, the city enjoyed a gilded age through to the 1950s, its hothouse atmosphere captured vividly in Lawrence Durrell's *Alexandria Quartet*. Now somewhat provincial and down-at-heel despite a facelift, the city possesses little glamour and few ancient sites, but Alexandria's situation is charming, and its past still haunts the fading streets. Very crowded in summer, it is better in winter.

Abu el Abbas and Bouseiri Mosques

The domes and minarets of these adjacent mosques lend a graceful touch to the skyline of the Eastern Harbour (*see p73*). The larger of the two is the Abu el Abbas Mosque, built in 1943 over a 13th-century tomb. Around it clusters the picturesque old quarter. Between it and the Corniche is the Bouseiri

Mosque, twinkling with lights at night. *Overlooking the Corniche towards Qaytbay Fort. 2km (1¼ miles) northwest of Midan Sa'ad Zaghloul. Open: dawn until late. Free admission.*

Anfushi tombs

Cut into the limestone ridge that formed the island of Pharos, these four tombs are basically Greek with Egyptian elements. The walls are painted to give the impression of marble and tile. In the tomb furthest to the right there are scenes of a *felucca*, and a warship of the type Cleopatra might have used to sail into Actium. *At the western end of Sharia Ras el Tin. 2.5km (1½ miles) northwest of Midan Sa'ad Zaghloul. Open: daily 9am–4pm. Closed: Fri 11.30am–1.30pm. Admission charge.*

Attarine

There is everything from old postcards to antique furniture to fascinate you in this flea market area of Alexandria, which centres on Sharia el Attarine. *Sharia el Attarine runs south from Sharia Sidi el Mitwalli. 1km (2⁄3 mile) south of Midan Sa'ad Zaghloul. Shops open until 9pm. Closed: Sun.*

Bibliotheca Alexandrina

This great library is a testament to a unique ecumenical effort. With three museums, five research institutes, several exhibition galleries, a planetarium and a huge number of books, this is a beautiful, symbolic and distinctive landmark.

On the Corniche at El Shatby.
Tel: (203) 483 9999.
e-mail: visits@biblex.org

Coptic Orthodox Cathedral of St Mark

The interior of the church is handsome. Note the plaque listing all the Coptic patriarchs, going right back to St Mark, said to be the traditional founder of Christianity in Egypt.

Rue de l'Eglise Copte, west along Sharia Sa'ad Zaghloul from Sharia el Nebi Danyal. 400m (440yds) southwest from Midan Sa'ad Zaghloul. Open: early morning until late. Free admission.

Graeco-Roman Museum

Filling the historical gap between the Egyptian Antiquities Museum and the Coptic Museum, both in Cairo, the Graeco-Roman Museum covers the fascinating period when Western culture overlaid and sometimes incorporated the native Egyptian world. Its spacious and uncluttered rooms are arranged around a central garden, making it a pleasant place to linger. Many of the exhibits are from Alexandria and its vicinity; the rest are from other areas of Greek settlement – the Delta, the Faiyûm and Middle Egypt.

Note the statue of Serapis in Room 6. This jolly-looking god, who combined the human look of Dionysios with the cult of the Apis bull, was invented by the Ptolemies in an effort to unite Greek and Egyptian culture.

The finest objects in the museum are the small Tanagra terracotta figures in Room 18A, dating from late 4th-century to early 2nd-century BC Alexandrian tombs of children, adolescents and young women. Closed for renovation.

One of the great cities of antiquity, Alexandria is Egypt's largest port

Sharia Mathaf, north off Sharia Horreya. 1km (²/₃ mile) east of Midan Sa'ad Zaghloul. Open: daily 9am–4pm. Closed: Fri 11.30am–1.30pm. Admission charge.

Kom el Dikka

This area near the centre of Alexandria has revealed a Roman odeon (a theatre for musical performances) and a large complex of 3rd-century AD Roman baths. The site gives you an idea of how much of the ancient city could be recovered – if only the modern city were knocked down.

Entrance on the south side of the large square, Midan el Gumhuriya, in front of the railway station. 1km (²/₃ mile) southeast of Midan Sa'ad Zaghloul. Open: daily 9am–4pm. Closed: Fri 11.30am–1.30pm. Admission charge.

Kom el Shogafa Catacombs

The largest and weirdest tombs in Alexandria (*see p72*).

West off Sharia Amud el Sawari. 2.5km (1¹/₂ miles) south of Midan Sa'ad Zaghloul. Open: daily 9am–4pm. Closed: Fri 11.30am–1.30pm. Admission charge.

Montazah Palace and Gardens

Built in Turko-Florentine style at the end of the 19th century by the Khedive Abbas II, this was the royal summer residence. Notice the letter F used as a recurring motif outside. A fortune teller had told King Fuad that the letter would bring his family luck. So he and his son Farouk gave all their children

names beginning with F. But in 1951, Farouk married Narriman and neglected to change her name. In January 1952 she bore him a son, Ahmed Fuad, the F relegated to second place. Six months later King Farouk was out of a job.

16km (10 miles) northeast of Midan Sa'ad Zaghloul. Gardens open: 24 hours daily. Admission charge.

National Museum

Built in Italian style in 1928, the museum was first owned by the American Embassy then bought by the Supreme Council of Antiquities in 1996. There are some 1,800 pieces here, telling the history of the people of Alexandria from antiquity to modern times.

110 Horreya Road. Open: daily 9am–4pm. Closed: Fri 11.30am–1.30pm.

Pompey's Pillar

The Alexandrian acropolis once stood here (*see p72*).

Sharia Amud el Sawari. 2km (1¹/₄ miles) south of Midan Sa'ad Zaghloul. Open: daily 9am–4pm. Closed: Fri 11.30am–1.30pm. Admission charge.

Qaytbay Fort

The fort stands on the site of the famous Ptolemaic lighthouse (*see p73*).

At the tip of the western arm of the Eastern Harbour. 3.5km (2¹/₄ miles) northwest of Midan Sa'ad Zaghloul. Open: 9am–4pm. Closed: Fri 11.30am–1.30pm. Admission charge.

Carriage ride: Alexandria

Carriages, which can comfortably take two people, are the most delightful way to travel around Alexandria. Tell the driver where you wish to go.

By taxi, this tour will take you at least 3 hours.

Begin outside the Cecil Hotel on the Corniche at Midan Sa'ad Zaghloul.

1 The Cecil Hotel

This Moorish pile, built in 1929, is something of a landmark. Somerset Maugham, Noël Coward, and Lawrence Durrell have all signed its visitors' book. Take time to refresh yourself in its Art Deco tea lounge. Outside once stood the **Caesareum**, which Cleopatra built as a temple dedicated to Mark Antony. There perhaps she committed suicide, and from there came Cleopatra's Needle, now in London, and the obelisk in New York's Central Park.

Head southwest to where Pompey's Pillar and Kom el Shogafa are close together.

2 Pompey's Pillar

Wrongly attributed by the Crusaders to the 1st-century BC Roman general Pompey, the pillar was raised at the end of the 3rd century AD to the emperor Diocletian. At its base are two pink granite sphinxes of the Ptolemaic period. This was once the city's acropolis, and here also stood the Temple of Serapis, a Graeco-Egyptian god invented by the Ptolemies. The temple was destroyed by a Christian mob in AD 391.

A short ride south is Kom el Shogafa.

3 Kom el Shogafa Catacombs

This largest Roman funerary complex in Egypt dates from the 2nd century AD. A winding staircase leads to an underground rotunda encircled by sarcophagi. Next to it is the banqueting hall where relatives of the deceased saw them out with a feast. At the level below is the central tomb chamber, decorated in a weird blend of classical and Egyptian styles. Inside stand dog-headed Anubis and crocodile-headed Sobek, both dressed as Roman centurions (*see p71*).

Head north to Midan el Tahrir.

4 Midan el Tahrir to Fort Qaytbay

In the square is an equestrian statue of Mohammed Ali, who brought Alexandria back to life in the 19th century. In Alexander's time, a causeway was built to the island of Pharos. Long ago silted up, its line is followed by Sharia Faransa running from the north-west corner of Midan el Tahrir through the picturesque old Egyptian quarter.

Towards the Western Harbour are the **Anfushi tombs** (*see p69*), while on the headland overlooking the harbour is **Ras el Tin Palace** (the gardens are open to the public). Here, on 26 July 1952, King Farouk abdicated, sailing into exile.

5 Qaytbay Fort

The present 15th-century fort was built by Sultan Qaytbay from fragments of

the six-times taller Pharos lighthouse, which had been destroyed by earthquakes. Renowned as one of the seven wonders of the ancient world, the Pharos could, by means of a mirror, direct a beam of sunlight, or the light of a fire, far out to sea (*see p71*).

6 Along the Corniche

Follow the Eastern Harbour back towards the Cecil Hotel, passing on your right the modern mosque of **Bouseiri** and, behind it, **Abu el Abbas** (*see p69*).

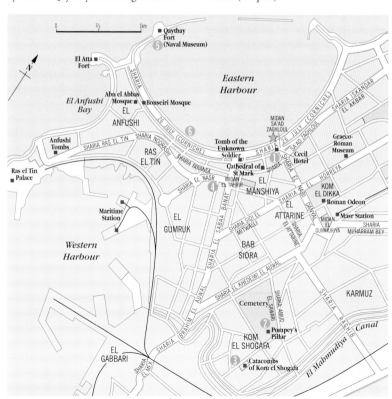

Excursions from Alexandria

Abusir

The name Abusir contains, in transmuted form, the memory of a small ancient city, Taposiris. Although the site is interesting and simple to get to, few people visit it as it is little known.

Taposiris stood at the western end of the same limestone ridge upon which Alexandria was built. Its ruins are slight, except for its tower and its temple. The enclosure walls of its **Temple of Osiris** are impressive, and there are pylons to climb for fine views over the delicate green marshes of Lake Maryut, which lies to the south.

To the north the sea is astonishingly turquoise against the burning white coastal sand. The interior of the temple has disappeared, except for the foundations of an early church.

A few hundred metres to the east stands the tower, in fact a Roman lighthouse, built on the same pattern but one-tenth the size of the Pharos. *Along the Mediterranean coast road. 45km (28 miles) west of Alexandria, unprotected, always open and free. A hired car or taxi is needed to get here.*

El Alamein

The scene of the famous series of World War II battles is now marked by a museum with tanks and pieces of heavy artillery, while immediately to the east of the village is the starkly beautiful British Cemetery. The Italian and German cemeteries are respectively 8km (5 miles) and 12km (7 ^{1}/$_2$ miles) further west.

On 17 July 1942, British General Auchinleck stopped Rommel's advance on Alexandria. Over the period 23 October to 5 November 1942, British Field Marshal Montgomery decisively defeated the Germans and put Rommel on the run. Within little more than six months the Germans and Italians were cleared from Africa altogether.

On the Mediterranean coast road. 106km (66 miles) west of Alexandria. Museum open: daily 9am–6pm, but closes at 3pm during Ramadan. Admission charge. Buses stop here between Alexandria and Mersa Matruh, but, although you can reserve a seat from Alexandria, you cannot at El Alamein, and will probably have to stand during the return journey. A hired car or taxi would be more practical.

Mersa Matruh

While en route to the oasis of Siwa (*see p63*), you might wish to pause here for

Memorials to three famous commanders at El Alamein

the magnificent beaches outside this one-time fishing port, now something of a boom town.

On the coast, 290km (180 miles) west of Alexandria. Service taxis and fast non-stop buses make the journey in 4 hours, while buses stopping at El Alamein and Sîdi Abd el Rahman take 5 hours.

Rashid (Rosetta)

Founded in the 9th century AD, Rosetta flourished as Alexandria declined. During the 17th and 18th centuries, it was Egypt's most important port. Many of its houses have been restored, and constitute the finest examples in Egypt of Islamic domestic architecture outside the capital, Cairo.

With the 19th-century refounding of Alexandria, Rosetta has in turn declined and is now a small agricultural market and fishing town, pleasantly situated on the western arm of the Nile, 10km (6 miles) from the sea. The town is most famously associated with the discovery here by one of Napoleon's soldiers of the **Rosetta Stone**, now in the British Museum. Because its inscription in ancient hieroglyphics is repeated in Greek, in 1821 Jean François Champollion succeeded in deciphering the ancient Egyptian language, thereby opening up Egypt's pharaonic past.

65km (40 miles) east of Alexandria. Both buses and service taxis make the trip.

Sîdi Abd el Rahman

This is a resort with a beautiful white beach. Accommodation is almost impossible to book during summer, but you might like to stop here for a swim when visiting El Alamein.

On the Mediterranean coast. 26km (16 miles) west of El Alamein, 132km (82 miles) west of Alexandria. Though buses and service taxis stop here, there is likely to be standing room only on the bus back to Alexandria.

Fishing boats off Rashid

East of the Nile and the Red Sea Coast

To travel east of the Nile is to enter another world. The level, green and placid landscapes of Egypt's river and its Delta are left behind. Instead, mountains line the Red Sea coast, while central and southern Sinai are harsh and rocky, as though in a state of geological eruption. There is also the remarkable sight of the Suez Canal, the ceaseless passage of ships like patrols along a border.

The impression of arriving at a frontier is due to a great rip in the earth's surface which extends from Africa's Rift Valley in the south to the valley of the River Jordan in the north. The **Red Sea** is extremely deep and its coastal mountains in the Sinai peninsula rise over 2,000m (6,560ft). Along with its northern finger, the **Gulf of Aqaba**, its enclosed waters are exceptionally warm and settled, encouraging the formation of coral reefs. The Gulf also attracts many brilliantly coloured fish that make this one of the finest underwater panoramas in the world for adventurous scuba divers.

Sinai, too, offers adventure, not only along its coasts, but for off-road enthusiasts wishing to explore its vast sandscapes in the north, and the wild mountains and *wadis* of its central and southern interior. Tradition claims that Moses wandered among the jagged peaks in the south, an area of enormous historic significance, which accounts for the presence here of one of the most magnificent of all monasteries, that of St Catherine's, cradled at the foot of a dramatic outcrop of Mt Sinai (*see p80*).

El Arîsh

Originally, El Arîsh was merely a Bedouin settlement on the Mediterranean coast of Sinai. Now it is the largest town on the peninsula with several hotels along its magnificent palm-fringed beach.

On Sinai's northern coast road. 278km (173 miles) northeast of Cairo via Ismailia and the Suez Canal ferry crossing at Qantara. Alternatively, you can travel via the tunnel north of Suez, in which case the Cairo-El Arîsh distance totals 437km (273 miles). There are also flights from Cairo.

Dahab

On the east coast of Sinai, and beautifully set against a backdrop of mountains, Dahab was once the hippy colony of Egypt. Although still a draw to a young crowd, it also has a sophisticated side and its great attraction is the reef fish. It's an excellent spot for water sports and windsurfing and is famous for its deep dive sites.

494km (307 miles) from Cairo via the Suez Tunnel. The bus takes 8 hours. There are flights from Cairo to Sharm el Sheikh.

Feiran Oasis

The Feiran Oasis, the largest in Sinai, is like a secret garden of palms, tamarisks and wheat set between towering mountain walls. Monks and hermits lived in the oasis during the early Christian centuries. Amid a plantation here, an avenue of column drums and capitals salvaged from ancient buildings leads up to a 19th-century chapel dedicated to Moses. Behind it are the ruins of a 4th-century bishop's palace.

South-central Sinai. 250km (155 miles) from the Suez tunnel en route to St Catherine's Monastery, and 395km (245 miles) east of Cairo (5½ hours by bus).

Hurghada

Once a fishing village, Hurghada is now a thriving, small city mainly dedicated to tourism. It has a variety of resort hotels stretching several kilometres to the north and south of the city. These have clean, private beaches and are often totally self-sufficient. The town has an aquarium, but you should really hire a boat to the islands and reefs,

where you can submerge yourself in the crystalline waters to enjoy a brilliantly coloured submarine world.

On the Red Sea coast road. 406km (252 miles) south of Suez, 550km (342 miles) southeast of Cairo (7 hours by bus) and 235km (146 miles) northeast of Luxor. Flights from Cairo and Luxor. The aquarium is on Sharia el Bahr. Open: daily 9am–10pm. Admission charge.

El Gouna

El Gouna is an attractive, purpose-built resort north of Hurghada on the Red Sea. It has a number of hotels and resorts to suit all pockets and has, in fact, much more to recommend it than Hurghada.

25km (15½ miles) north of Hurghada, accessible by shuttle bus from Hurghada.

For off-road destinations in Sinai and the Red Sea mountains, *see pp128–9*; for more on the Red Sea resorts, *see pp142–3*.

Travelling in the harsh Sinai environment

Sharia el Gumhuriya, Port Said

Nuweiba

Less attractively situated than Dahab, and somewhat quieter, Nuweiba has a few diving facilities for exploring its fine reefs.

On the Gulf of Aqaba, on the eastern coast of Sinai. The distance from Cairo via the Suez tunnel is 560km (348 miles). The bus takes 8½ hours. There are flights from Cairo to Sharm el Sheikh.

Ismailia

Midway along the Suez Canal, Ismailia is its operational headquarters. The town owes its character to the British, and its waterside district of wide, clean streets with suburban-style houses in well-planted gardens looks remarkably like a tropical England. The town museum exhibits recall ancient attempts to dig the canal. That job was finally accomplished in the 1860s under the direction of Ferdinand de Lesseps, whose house is on the main street as you come in from Cairo. On the canal there is a club with a sandy beach, deck chairs and refreshments, and hypnotic views of supertankers parading by.

128km (80 miles) northeast of Cairo, served by trains, buses and service taxis. Museum open: daily 9am–4pm. Closed: Fri 11am–2pm. Admission charge. De Lesseps' House not generally open without permission from Suez Canal Authority.

Port Said

At the north end of the Suez Canal and with town beaches along the Mediterranean, Port Said prospered owing to its duty-free status. Along

MOSES AND THE EXODUS

How much, if any, of the story of the Exodus is historical is a matter of debate. Scholars accept that the Old Testament account was written by persons unknown, anything up to 1,000 years after the late second-millennium BC events described.

According to biblical tradition, Moses led the Children of Israel from Pi-Ramses in the Delta via the Red Sea, which obediently parted so they could walk across into Sinai. There, God gave Moses the Ten Commandments on top of a mountain, associated with Gebel Musa (Mount Sinai) near St Catherine's Monastery, which also claims possession of the Burning Bush. Moses made a Covenant with God atop Mount Sinai, promising him that the Israelites would obey the Ten Commandments. The Israelites wandered the Sinai for 40 years before finally entering the Promised Land.

Sharia el Gumhuriya, two streets back from the canal, there are many beautiful old wooden buildings with balconies. The **National Museum** is closed at the moment, but the small **Military Museum** is worth a visit. The town's most famous landmark is the Suez Canal Building. Overlooking the canal itself, its gleaming white colonnade is crowned with three brilliant green domes. One way of getting a good view of the canal is to take the commuter ferry over to Port Fuad, a voyage from Africa to Asia.
200km (124 miles) northeast of Cairo, via Ismailia (4 hours). National Museum closed. Military Museum open: 9am–2pm, 7.30–8.30pm (10am–1pm Fri). Admission charge.

St Antony's Monastery (Deir Anba Antunius)

Surrounded by 2km (1¹/₄ miles) of walls standing 12m (39ft) high, St Antony's Monastery is dramatically set against the cliffs of the Eastern Desert plateau. St Antony, who died in AD 356, is the world's first historically documented Christian hermit, and the inspiration for the monastic movement. This monastery, founded by his disciples, claims to be the earliest in the world. Once rivalling the Greek Orthodox Monastery of St Catherine in beauty, it was sacked by Bedouins in the 15th century, but retains the parapets of the 10th-century walls, the 16th-century four-storey keep, and numerous frescoes of prophets and saints inside the 12th-century church. Against the south wall is the Spring of St Antony, while a 2km (1¹/₄-mile) path climbs up behind the monastery to St Antony's Cave.
On the Red Sea coast road, 120km (75 miles) south of Suez; follow the road inland for 30km (18¹/₂ miles) before turning south for 10km (6 miles) to the monastery.
There is no public transport.

The old grain mill, St Antony's Monastery

St Catherine's Monastery
(Deir Sant Katerin)

There are few more dramatic sights in Egypt than the tranquil Monastery of St Catherine against the flank of Mount Sinai. You approach from what is claimed to be the plain of Raha, where the wandering Israelites worshipped the golden calf, while above you looms the 2,285m (7,497ft) mountain where Moses is said to have received the Ten Commandments from God.

Built in about AD 530, the monastery is Greek Orthodox, its monks mostly from Crete and Cyprus. Protected by its fortress-like walls, and respected by Jews, Christians and Muslims alike

St Catherine's Monastery under Mount Sinai

for its associations with Moses, St Catherine's Monastery has generally enjoyed the peace and patronage denied to Coptic monasteries, so that it preserves today all the splendour of its Byzantine past.

Outside its gate stands the Charnel House, heaped high with the bones of monks under the inattentive gaze of St Stephen the Porter, a 6th-century monk, dressed in a purple robe and holding a staff in his skeletal hand.

Dominating the interior of the monastery is the Church of the Transfiguration. Through the magnificently carved 6th-century inner doors of the narthex you enter the vast nave. At its far end is a gilded iconostasis adorned with large icons of John the Baptist, Mary, Jesus and St Catherine, all 17th-century Cretan work. To the right, behind the iconostasis, is the reliquary which is said to contain St Catherine's skull and left hand. In the apse of the church is the 6th-century mosaic of the Transfiguration, one of the finest works of Byzantine art. Its subject is taken from *Matthew 17:1–3*. After Jesus had asked his disciples who they thought he was, he '. . . was transfigured before them: and his face did shine as the sun, and his raiment was white as the light.' On either side of the windows above the apse are mosaics of Moses taking off his sandals before the Burning Bush and receiving the Ten Commandments. Some of the monastery's 5,000 icons are displayed in the Icon Gallery next to the Library, which has a valuable collection of books and manuscripts, some dating to the 5th century AD.

A winding path climbs up Mount Sinai from behind the monastery. If you wish to have the mountain to yourself, wait until later in the day; but traditionally, visitors leave at 2am, allowing 2 hours for the climb, in order to reach the summit by sunrise. It can be cold, but the dawn is magnificent and the early-morning light superb for photography. The walk is fine for any halfway fit person, and the route is easy to follow in the dark. As an alternative, you can hire a camel at the bottom. When visiting the monastery, please dress modestly. You will not be allowed in if incorrectly dressed and there is no supply of coverings.

In southern Sinai. 443km (275 miles) from Cairo. Buses take 6 hours. There are also flights and tours. Open: Mon–Thur & Sat 9am–noon. Closed: Fri, Sun, holidays and some fasting days. Check with Representative Office in Cairo. Tel: (202) 4828513. Free admission.

Sharm el Sheikh, Na'ama Bay and Ras Muhammad

Sharm el Sheikh and Na'ama Bay, 7km (4^1/$_4$ miles) north, are twin resorts on Sinai's eastern coast. Sharm is popular with tourists, and together with Na'ama Bay is the bustling centre of activity. New resorts have sprung up along the coast to north and south with good accommodation and facilities for divers and non-divers. From Sharm you can take a boat to Ras Muhammad, a

The resort of Sharm el Sheikh

marine National Park at the southernmost tip of Sinai, where there are superb views across the Gulf of Suez to the Red Sea mountains and across the Gulf of Aqaba to Saudi Arabia. But most spectacular are its underwater views, though the sea can be rough out at the reefs, where diving is not really suitable for beginners. Everyone, however, can enjoy the underwater snorkelling.

514km (319 miles) southeast from Cairo. Buses, stopping at Sharm and Na'ama Bay, take 6 hours. There are flights to Sharm from Cairo and Hurghada, and a ferry sails between Sharm and Hurghada. There is no public transport to Ras Muhammad other than boat trips from Sharm. Admission charge.

Suez

Badly affected by the 1967 and 1973 wars with Israel and the sporadic shelling in between, Suez is now a largely rebuilt industrial centre. The Ahmed Hamdi Tunnel, 12km (7^1/$_2$ miles) north, is the main route for traffic into Sinai.

134km (83 miles) east of Cairo, reached by trains, buses and service taxis.

The Suez Canal

The idea of a canal to link the Red Sea with the Mediterranean is by no means a modern concept. The earliest historically authenticated attempt was made by Necho, a 26th-Dynasty pharaoh, who abandoned the project when an oracle warned that only the Persians would benefit from it. Indeed, it was the Persian King Darius I who completed it a century later, in about 500 BC.

The first canal ran from the Red Sea to about where present-day Ismailia stands, before turning westwards to Bubastis, near modern Zagazig, to join up with a now vanished arm of the Nile. It was maintained by the Ptolemies and the Romans, but was abandoned by the Arabs.

The present canal, at 167km (104 miles), is the third longest in the world, and the longest without locks. Its completion in 1869, under the direction of the Frenchman Ferdinand de Lesseps, was a great feat for Egypt and of major importance to world trade. That narrow strip of water saved shipping from the States and Canada, Britain and Europe having to travel the length of Africa, cutting thousands of kilometres off their journey. It opened up trade to parts

The Suez Canal – one of the world's most vital passages for trade

A container ship on the Suez Canal

of the world previously restricted, and brought invaluable revenue to Egypt.

Nasser's nationalisation of the foreign-owned Suez Canal Company in 1956 was a reaction to nearly a century of direct or indirect Western rule. This led to the Suez Crisis, an attack on Egypt by Britain, France and Israel, called off after Soviet and American objections. It was one of the most tense and dangerous moments of the Cold War. The 1967 war with Israel closed the canal for eight years, and the shelling of the canal towns during that time caused enormous damage.

In 1975 President Sadat reopened the canal. As many as 50 ships pass through every 24 hours with an average transit time of 15 hours. They carry with them a significant amount of the world's trade, and the fees they pay are a major income-earner for Egypt. A new bridge links East and West, making the crossing from mainland Egypt to Sinai easier.

The Nile Valley:
Cairo to Luxor

Throughout Egyptian history a distinction has been made between Lower Egypt, which is the land of the Delta, and Upper Egypt, where the desert and mountains encroach upon the Nile Valley with its narrow band of cultivation. Lower Egypt, then and now, has been more cosmopolitan, more exposed to foreign influences. From Upper Egypt have come periodic bursts of conservative reaction.

Ancient Memphis and now Cairo stand near the junction of the Delta and the Nile Valley, but the sense of entering Upper Egypt only really begins when you have got beyond Beni Suef, a busy and unattractive town 124km (77 miles) south of Cairo. From this point, you are leaving behind those most impressive monuments of the Old Kingdom at Gîza and Saqqâra. The Nile Valley is more associated with later pharaonic periods, though along this first stretch of the river, heavily populated by Copts, there are also several interesting early Christian sites.

Abydos

Ancient Abydos was the shrine of Osiris, who, as god of the underworld, was also a central figure in the Egyptians' notions of resurrection and the afterlife. The 19th-Dynasty New Kingdom pharaoh Seti I, though possessing a mortuary temple in the Theban necropolis, built one here as well. Reacting against Akhenaton's revolution in worship and art (*see opposite*), Seti was determined to reinstate Egyptian style as it had existed during the Old Kingdom.

The first hypostyle hall was decorated after Seti's death by his son, Ramses II. The more finely carved and coloured work on the walls of the second hypostyle hall (some of the finest reliefs to be seen anywhere in Egypt) were executed during Seti's lifetime. They

Relief carving on entrance pillar

include profiles of Seti himself, which closely resemble the distinctive features of his mummy at the Museum of Egyptian Antiquities in Cairo (*see p40*).

At the left of the second hypostyle hall is a passageway known as the Gallery of the Kings for its cartouches of Seti's predecessors back to the time of Menes. This has proved invaluable to Egyptologists in determining the correct order of pharaonic succession. Adjacent reliefs show Seti and his son, the future Ramses II, revering their ancestors.

600km (373 miles) south of Cairo, on the west bank of the Nile. 10km (6 miles) southwest of El Balyana, which is 40km (25 miles) northwest of Nag Hammâdi. Several Cairo–Luxor trains stop at El Balyana, from where service taxis run out to Abydos. Alternatively, take a tour or hire a taxi from Luxor, visiting both Abydos and Dendera. These are also *covered by some cruises. It is likely that you will travel in a police convoy or with an escort. Open: 7am–5pm. Admission charge.*

OSIRIS AND ATON

The cult of Osiris formed part of the orthodox religion of ancient Egypt. The story goes that Osiris, son of Re, was a king who ruled justly and was greatly loved in distant times. Isis was his sister and wife, and Seth was his brother. When Seth killed Osiris and dismembered his body, Isis searched out the pieces and put them together again. Abydos, where Isis found Osiris' head, became a national shrine. Just as she restored him to life in the underworld, so all who followed the Osiris cult would share in the promise of resurrection and eternal life.

The 18th-Dynasty pharaoh Akhenaton rejected both the priesthood of Amun at Thebes and the Osiris cult, and was called a heretic. At Amarna, he worshipped instead the Aton, the solar disc, to whom he wrote a hymn, which is found in many of the Amarna tombs.

The Nile Valley: Cairo to Luxor

Atmospheric Abydos, sacred to the memory of Osiris, the god of resurrection

Asyût

The largest town in Upper Egypt and home to an Islamic university, Asyût has long been a centre for fundamentalist activity. There have been sporadic outbursts of violence against the security forces and against tourists, and a strong military presence is maintained. Now it is relatively peaceful.

378km (235 miles) south of Cairo. Buses depart from here for the oases of the Western Desert.

Beni Hasan

A path leads up from the east bank of the Nile to 39 Middle Kingdom tombs cut into the cliff face, though only four are normally open to the public. These tombs belonged to provincial governors and are exceptional for the detail of their paintings which depict agriculture, craft, hunting and sports, along with occasional military scenes.

On the east bank of the Nile. 275km (171 miles) south of Cairo and 25km (15¹/₂ miles) south of El Minya. A taxi from El Minya will take you to the ferry landing; on your return it can take you on to Amarna. Be prepared for a police escort or convoy. Open: 8am–5pm. Admission charge.

Dendera

For the ancient Egyptians, the goddess of joy and love was Hathor, the cow goddess, whose name means Castle of Horus. As a fertility goddess she suckled Horus, the son of Isis and Osiris, and then lay with him at Edfu. Each year a great pageant takes place at her temple at Dendera.

Every dynasty legitimised itself by identifying with various aspects of the Osiris story, and the Ptolemies were no exception. This **Temple of Hathor** at Dendera is their construction, and,

Detailed wall paintings at Beni Hasan throw light on everyday life in Egypt

The magnificent site at Dendera

a magnificent relief of Nut, the sky goddess, giving birth to the sun, whose rays illuminate Hathor. On the roof is the elegant kiosk where Hathor was exposed to the sun's revivifying force, while above the stairwells are the twin chapels of Osiris, their decorations including a zodiac (though the original has been removed to the Louvre, Paris). Colossal reliefs on the outside rear wall of the temple show Caesarion, son of Julius Caesar, with his mother, the great Cleopatra, and last of the Ptolemies. *618km (384 miles) south of Cairo, on the west bank of the Nile. 4km (2 1/2 miles) west of Qena. From the train station you can take a taxi or carriage to the temple. Alternatively, take a tour or hire a taxi from Luxor, visiting both Dendera and Abydos, which are also sometimes covered by cruises. Be prepared to join a convoy. Temple open: 7am–6pm. Admission charge.*

later, even the Romans took a hand, adding the pylon-shaped façade with its six Hathor-headed columns.

You pass through a succession of halls which become smaller, lower and darker, until you reach the inner sanctuary of the goddess. Normally kept bolted and in darkness, it was opened and illuminated by torchlight to allow Hathor's adoration by the pharaoh. This ritual is depicted on wall reliefs inside.

At the New Year, images of the goddess were carried up to the roof where they made contact with the rays of Re – a spiritual emergence from darkness into light. You can retrace the route by climbing the stairways from within the temple, their walls incised with reliefs illustrating the procession. Near the base of the west stairway is the New Year Chapel. On its ceiling is

El Minya

Within easy reach of Beni Hasan and Amarna, El Minya, which has a large Christian community, has unfortunately taken over from Asyût as a centre for unrest, and suffers from sporadic outbursts of violence. Nevertheless, its warm and friendly population enjoys promenading along its winding riverside corniche, while amid overgrown gardens stand charming villas, once the homes of Greek and Egyptian cotton magnates. *On the west bank of the Nile. 250km (155 miles) south of Cairo.*

MONASTERIES ALONG THE NILE
Burnt Monastery (Deir el Muharraq)

Unusually, this flourishing Coptic monastery is not far off in the desert but just within the cultivated zone. By tradition this marks the southernmost point in the flight of the Holy Family. Here, it is said, Joseph heard the angel's words as recorded in St Matthew's Gospel: 'Arise, and take the young child and his mother, and go into the land of Israel.' A church dating back at least to the 8th century and dedicated to the Virgin, El Adra, stands over the cave where the Holy Family supposedly stayed. Next to it is a 12th-century keep. Annually, during the week of 21 June, more than 50,000 people collect here to attend the Feast of the Consecration of the Church of the Virgin.

On the west bank of the Nile. About 30km (18¹/₂ miles) south of the ferry crossing for Amarna, 80km (50 miles) south of El Minya, and 40km (25 miles) north of Asyût. A taxi tour could be included in a tour of Beni Hasan and Amarna. For details on Coptic monasteries, see p178.

White Monastery (Deir el Abyad)

As you follow the road out from Sohâg you see a startling sight. At the edge of the cultivation, with its back against the hills of the desert plateau, stands what seems to be an intact Egyptian temple. This is known as the White Monastery, and is the most remarkable instance

Original bust of Queen Nefertiti

of the similarity between Coptic and pharaonic architecture.

Massive white limestone walls slope inwards and are finished off with a cavetto cornice of white marble. Inside is an enormous basilical church. To call it a monastery is misleading, for the ruins of that once vast structure housing over 2,000 monks now lie beneath the mounds of rubble outside. The surviving building is in fact a fortified monastery church built in about AD 440 by St Shenute, whose *moulid* is celebrated here during the week leading up to 14 July.

The nave is in ruins – much of the damage was caused by Mamelukes fleeing Napoleon's troops in 1798. Nevertheless, the proportions of the church, both the exterior and interior, and the broken columns of marble and black granite make a noble impression. What was the sanctuary has been bricked off to form a complete church, its apses arranged as a trefoil, with 12th-century paintings adorning their semidomes.

Sohâg is 470km (292 miles) south of Cairo. From there a taxi can take you the 5km (3 miles) west to the White Monastery. Open: daily 7am–6pm; all night during the moulid. Free admission.

Tell el Amarna

When the 18th-Dynasty pharaoh Akhenaton broke with the worship of Amun at Thebes in favour of the sun disc Aton (*see p85*), he founded his new capital Akhetaton ('Resting Place of the Disc') at the place now called Tell el Amarna, or simply, Amarna. The city was abandoned after the deaths of Akhenaton and his beautiful queen Nefertiti. Thebes once again became the capital, and a compliant

Tutankhamun was persuaded to reinstate the worship of Amun.

Only the merest traces of palaces, temples and houses remain in this great sand-filled crescent between the Nile and the cliffs of the Eastern Desert. The cliff-face tombs offer a splendid view back over the plain.

There is a lonely and melancholy beauty to Amarna, but for its paintings, reliefs and sculptures you must visit the Museum of Egyptian Antiquities in Cairo (*see p40*).

On the east bank of the Nile. 314km (195 miles) south of Cairo and 67km (42 miles) south of El Minya. From El Minya, take a taxi to the west-bank ferry landing and cross over to the village of El Till. The site lies behind the village. Access is unrestricted and free. At the village you can hire donkeys or a tractor to visit the tombs, 4km (2 1/2 miles) east. For all excursions, be prepared to join a convoy or have a police escort. Open: 7am–5pm. Admission charge.

A dusty track to the Tell el Amarna rock tombs is well worth the climb

The river of life

Journeying through Egypt by road or rail, you miss the grandeur of the Nile. It is only by air that you get a bird's-eye view of the mighty river, and the strip of cultivation to either side. However, when you sail for days along the Nile there is the clear sense that you are travelling along a valley, seeing sights that have not changed since time immemorial, a mixture of ancient and modern, biblical and secular.

In the early stages of the journey from Cairo to Aswân, the Nile cuts through rock and cliffs close on either side. These then fall away into the distance, and only fields can be seen, villages and vegetation, and people going about their daily life, washing their clothes and pots and pans in the river, children swimming and animals cooling down in the water.

Agriculture is very important to the economy of Egypt. Crops of all sorts are grown in the fertile Delta and along the cultivated strips either side of the Nile. There is sugar cane, maize and barseem, the clover fed to animals. Rice is grown, as is a variety of fruits and vegetables. Date palms proliferate, ranging from nearly black to pale yellow, either hard or soft, sweet or tart. Mango plantations and citrus groves are everywhere. At all times, one is reminded of how the river has forced its way through the arid desert and carved its passage through rock, bringing life to its banks. Life is also brought to the people of Egypt as a result of the trade on the Nile. Barges plough up and down the river, carrying their cargoes of stone and other valuable commodities which are cheaper to transport by river. *Feluccas* (*see pp132–3*) also ply their trade, not only in tourist towns and cities, but also as a means of transport from one side of the river to the other.

The pharaohs regarded the river with reverence, and their myths and beliefs are all interrelated. The Nile is indeed the artery of Egypt – a living, working river – the lifeline of the country today, as it was in the past.

The Nile, Africa's longest river, is the most picturesque record of Egyptian daily life

Luxor

The name Luxor is loosely applied by travellers to include three distinct places: the town of Luxor, with a population over 450,000, on the east bank of the Nile; the village of Karnak and its immense temple 4km (2¹/2 miles) north on the same bank; and the Theban necropolis on the west bank of the river opposite Luxor and Karnak. At the height of its glory during the 18th and 19th Dynasties, Thebes covered all of what is now Luxor and Karnak, and may have had a population as high as one million. Earlier, in Middle Kingdom times, its most important god had been Amun. When the Theban princes drove the alien Hyksos out of Lower Egypt and reunited the country, Thebes became capital of the New Kingdom, and Amun became Egypt's national god.

Apart from its military prowess, Thebes was also strategically situated between the agriculturally rich Delta and gold-rich Nubia. It is tempting to believe that the great pharaohs of the New Kingdom also responded to the beauty and never-failing fertility of the surrounding landscape.

It did inspire them to build, sometimes sensitively, sometimes

The bank of the Nile at Luxor

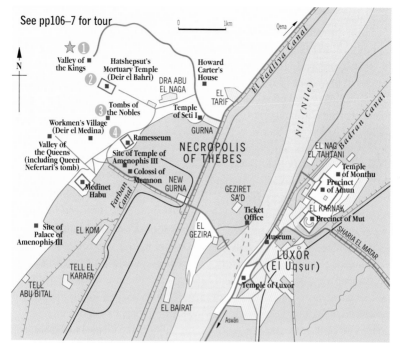

See pp106–7 for tour

grandiosely, and Thebes became the focus of an architectural activity so magnificent, and still well enough preserved, that it can lay just claim to being the world's greatest outdoor museum.

On the east bank, highlights include the Temple of Karnak, scene of the Sound and Light show, and the Luxor Temple (and Museum), which includes the Mosque of Haggag. The west bank highlights (in numbers on map) are covered by a taxi tour of the Theban necropolis (*see pp106–7*) which includes the Valley of the Kings, the Valley of the Queens, Hatshepsut's mortuary temple and the Colossi of Memnon.

VISITING THE WEST BANK

As soon as you arrive at the west bank of the Nile, buy tickets for the tombs and temples of the Theban necropolis that you want to visit that day. Generally, you will only be allowed to visit three tombs in the Valley of the Kings. Some are likely to be closed. Keep alternative choices in mind. You will not be allowed into the sites without a ticket and these are only valid on the day of issue. Tickets for Tutankhamun's tomb can only be purchased at the security gate entrance to the Valley of the Kings.

The ticket office is open from 6am–4pm. It is just up the road from the Colossi of Memnon statues for which you do not need a ticket. Tombs and temples are open 6am–6pm. All charge an admission fee. The west bank can be reached by taxi or tour bus by crossing Luxor Bridge, 8km (5 miles) south of the city centre. The ferry is not always available.

Colossi of Memnon

The mortuary temple of Amenophis III has vanished, and all that remains are the two famous colossi that once guarded its outer gates. They are gigantic statues of the enthroned Amenophis himself, and stand 19.5m (64ft) high. At one time they wore the royal crown and were even higher.

The one on the right (north) was shattered by an earthquake in 27 BC and later repaired; for nearly 200 years thereafter it would often emit a musical note as the sun rose over the eastern mountains. Greek and Roman tourists, including the emperor Hadrian in AD 130, camped overnight to witness the unusual phenomenon, and carved their names into the legs of the colossi.
On the west bank in the southern part of the necropolis. 3.5km (2¹/4 miles) from the Nile.

The Colossi of Memnon

'WONDERFUL THINGS!'

About his discovery of Tutankhamun's tomb, Howard Carter wrote: 'Details of the room within emerged slowly from the mist, strange animals, statues, and gold – everywhere the glint of gold. For the moment – an eternity it must have seemed to the others standing by – I was struck dumb with amazement, and when Lord Carnarvon, unable to stand the suspense any longer, enquired anxiously, "Can you see anything?", it was all I could do to get out the words, "Yes, wonderful things".'

Hatshepsut's Mortuary Temple (Deir el Bahri)

Hatshepsut's father, the 18th-Dynasty pharaoh Tuthmosis I, was the first to seek greater security for his mummified body by having a tomb dug in the Valley of the Kings. Hatshepsut followed his example, and ceremonies in her honour were held at her mortuary temple (*see p107*), built directly over her tomb chamber where she is thought to be buried. Early Christians used it as a monastery, which is why it is often known as Deir el Bahri, the Northern Monastery.

The temple has three terraces linked by ramps. The Lower Terrace was a garden with myrrh trees and fountains, as though giving a foretaste of life in the world beyond this one. Within the right colonnade that stands at the rear of the terrace, this theme is continued in delicate reliefs depicting an idealised country life. At the rear of the Middle Terrace, reliefs to the left, along the

Punt Colonnade, show Egyptians who had sailed south along the African coast to obtain myrrh trees for the temple being greeted by the chief of Punt and his extraordinarily corpulent wife. Reliefs along the Birth Colonnade to the right announce Hatshepsut's divine parentage. Her father as Amun sits opposite her mother Ahmosis, who is then led to the birth chamber.

As a female pharaoh, Hatshepsut was eager to underline the legitimacy of her rule, especially as it was being challenged by her stepson and nominal co-ruler, the future Tuthmosis III. When he finally came to the throne, following her death, he resentfully defaced her images here on the pillars of the Birth Colonnade and elsewhere, while preserving his own. The Upper Terrace, now restored, is still closed. *On the west bank, at the north end of the necropolis. 6km (4 miles) from the river. See panel on p93 for ticket details.*

Howard Carter's House (Qasr Carter)

On a barren hill overlooking the road which rises towards the Valley of the Kings is the large domed house where the archaeologist and artist Howard Carter lived during the time of his discovery of Tutankhamun's tomb. He had earlier worked for the Egyptian Exploration Fund, recording scenes from the walls of tombs and temples. *At the north end of the necropolis. 1km (²/₃ mile) north of Seti I's mortuary temple and 5km (3 miles) from the river. Closed to the public.*

Hatshepsut's Mortuary Temple (Deir el Bahri) rises out of the desert plain

Karnak

The Karnak site covers a huge area. The precinct of Amun in fact encloses several temples, but most people will be content to walk through the biggest of these, the Temple of Amun, the gigantic proportions of which are far larger than both St Paul's Cathedral in London and St Peter's Basilica in Rome.

One dynasty after another added to the Temple of Amun so that, from its founding during the Middle Kingdom to the building of its outermost or First Pylon during the 25th Dynasty, 1,300 years elapsed. The Asian conquests of Tuthmosis III and Ramses II brought New Kingdom Egypt to the peak of power and prosperity. The great god Amun also received his share, so that his temple soon controlled perhaps as much as a fifth of Egypt's workforce and owned nearly a third of its land.

Something of this story is told during the Sound and Light show which leads you briskly through part of the **Temple of Amun**, and deposits you on a seat in the grandstand overlooking the Sacred Lake.

By day you will have more of a chance to get your bearings. A processional way lined with ram-headed sphinxes leads into the temple. They represent Amun, and between the forelegs of each is a diminutive figure of the god's servant, Ramses II. The

First Pylon was built 600 years later. At 43m (141ft) high, it is the largest at Karnak, and nearly twice the size of the entrance pylon at the Temple of Luxor. A succession of pylons funnels you towards the sanctuary of the god.

Passing through the Second Pylon, you enter the Hypostyle Hall, the 19th-Dynasty work of Seti I and Ramses II. Its forest of columns is one of the most spectacular sights in Egypt. Each column is so massive that it takes the outstretched arms of six people to encircle one. Originally, the entire hall was roofed over. An obelisk raised by

SOUND AND LIGHT

On the east bank. 4km (2½ miles) north of Luxor. Open: daily 6am–6pm in summer; 5pm in winter. Admission charge. Sound and Light shows are held daily, with three or four performances during the course of the evening. They tell the story of Thebes, and some of the pharaohs, and at least one show per night is in English. The others alternate between French, German, Italian, Spanish, Japanese and Arabic. Admission charge.

Tuthmosis I stands in the small court between the Third and Fourth Pylons. Between the Fourth and Fifth Pylons stood two magnificent obelisks of Tuthmosis I's daughter, Hatshepsut. One has snapped in half; the upper portion lies at the northwest corner of the Sacred Lake where you can examine its fine hieroglyphic inscriptions. The other remains in place, and at 29.5m (97ft) is the tallest obelisk in Egypt. You will notice two pink granite pillars carved with lilies on one side and papyrus flowers on the other, the traditional symbols of Upper and Lower Egypt. Past these is the Sanctuary of the Sacred Boats, built in the time of Alexander the Great to replace the original. Along the south flank of the Temple of Amun is the Sacred Lake where the god's sacred boats took part in various ceremonies, culminating in the annual Opet festival when he sailed upriver to the Temple of Luxor. At its northwest corner, by part of Hatshepsut's obelisk, is a gigantic scarab dedicated to the rising sun.

The Avenue of Sphinxes before the First Pylon of the Temple of Amun

Luxor Museum

The museum contains a small but carefully selected number of beautifully displayed exhibits. Graeco-Roman, Coptic and Islamic artefacts are included, but the overwhelming emphasis is on the pharaonic period.

There are a few items from Tutankhamun's tomb, including a funerary bed, model boats and a golden cow's head. The other contents of his tomb are all in the Museum of Egyptian Antiquities in Cairo. Reliefs of Akhenaton and Nefertiti worshipping Aton, and scenes of their palace life are also displayed.

Most outstanding, however, are the black basalt and pink granite statues and busts of jug-eared Sesostris III of the 12th Dynasty, and of the 18th-Dynasty pharaohs Tuthmosis III,

Gilded cow's head, Luxor Museum

Amenophis II and Amenophis III. The craftsmanship is superb, and you can feel the sculptors' enjoyment of working with the graceful curves of crowns, necks and waists.

On the east bank, on Sharia Nahr el Nil. 1km (2/3 mile) north of the Temple of Luxor. Tel: (209) 2380269. Open: daily 9am–1pm & 5–9pm in winter; 9am–1pm & 5–10pm in summer. Admission charge.

Luxor Temple

Until the end of the 19th century, when excavations began, almost the whole of Luxor village stood within and on top of this debris-filled temple. Only the mosque of Abu Haggag was allowed to remain perched on top of its walls. Unlike Karnak, which was built over a long period of time, the Temple of Luxor is largely the work of the 18th-Dynasty pharaoh Amenophis III. With him began the fashion for gigantism that broadcasts the imperial pretensions of New Kingdom Egypt.

It was Ramses II, however, who later built the entrance pylons and the great court beyond. In front of the pylons he placed six colossal statues of himself, only three of which remain. Of the two obelisks he erected here, one was given to the French by Mohammed Ali and now stands in the Place de la Concorde in Paris. Incised on the pylons are scenes of the battle of Kadesh in Syria, which Ramses claimed as a victory against the Hittites, though he was lucky to escape from it with his life.

The vertical grooves on the pylons were made in order to support flagstaffs.

Numerous colossi of Ramses stand around the great court, his wife Nefertari knee-high at his side. On the far right-hand wall a relief shows the exterior of the temple, complete with colossi and obelisks, and banners waving from the pylons. From here, you enter the imposing colonnade of Amenophis III. On the right-hand wall are reliefs dating from the reign of Tutankhamun depicting the Opet festival, an annual fertility rite during which Amun sailed from Karnak for a conjugal reunion with his wife Mut, who resided at the Temple of Luxor with their son Khonsu. The Court of Amenophis leads to his Hypostyle Hall with interesting reliefs on its far walls showing his coronation by the gods.

These in turn lead on to the Sanctuary of the Sacred Boat of Amun, corresponding to the one at Karnak. Its inner chamber was rebuilt during the time of Alexander the Great. On the outside wall facing the river is a relief of a pharaonic-looking Alexander offering gifts to Amun who is in a state of presumably festive erection.

Returning through the temple and emerging again at the pylons, you notice the avenue of sphinxes that once led all the way to Karnak.

On the east bank, on Sharia Nahr el Nil at the centre of Luxor. Open: daily 6am–10pm, 9pm in winter. Admission charge. After dark, the temple is beautifully floodlit, creating a dramatic effect.

Putting Ramses II at Luxor Temple into perspective

Medînet Habu
(Mortuary Temple of Ramses III)

Ramses III's great mortuary temple is usually known as Medînet Habu, 'town of Habu'. During the Coptic period there was a town of some size, while part of the temple was used as a church.

Modelled closely on the Ramesseum, which had been built less than a century earlier, the temple of Ramses III is much better preserved, and is second in size only to the Temple of Amun at Karnak. It was, however, to prove the last major architectural work of the pharaonic period, as during the rest of the 20th Dynasty, Egypt's fortunes declined. You enter the site by a gatehouse which, judging from the reliefs on the walls of its upper storey, served as a resort where the pharaoh could amuse himself with the harem women. Straight ahead is the First Pylon which is worth climbing to gain an overall impression of temple layout, the pylons, columns and chambers becoming smaller and smaller as you gaze towards the sanctuary.

This was not only a mortuary temple, but also a royal residence. The First Court was the scene of ceremonies and entertainments, the pharaoh perhaps making appearances at the window in the left-hand wall which was also the palace façade. During the Ptolemaic and Roman periods, the Second Court was filled with houses and a church – the octagonal base of its font can be seen on the left. Beyond this are three hypostyle halls leading to the

Painting and relief carving in the Temple of Seti I and Ramses II at Abydos

sanctuary which once contained Amun's boat. Left off the Second Hypostyle Hall is the funerary chamber of Ramses III with depictions of Thoth inscribing the pharaoh's name.

If you now go back through the First Pylon and turn left, you can walk round to the outside wall of the temple to see its famous panoramic relief. This shows the attempted invasion of Egypt by the Sea Peoples, a coalition of northerners who had already overrun the Hittite empire in Anatolia (present-day Turkey) and Syria. They are shown arriving in ships and overland by ox-cart, bringing their families and all their belongings, attacking the Delta, and being repulsed by Ramses himself.

An inscription graphically describes the outcome: 'A net was prepared for them to ensnare them, those who entered into the rivermouths being confined and fallen within it, pinioned in their places, butchered and their corpses hacked up.'

On the west bank, at the southern end of the necropolis. 5km (3 miles) from the river.

Nobles' tombs

Hundreds of nobles' tombs have been found in the Theban necropolis. Two of the most interesting, those of Ramose and Sennufer, are described on page 107. Also worth visiting, if you have the time, are the tombs of Rekhmire, Menna, Nakht, Userhat and Khaemhat.

On the west bank near, and sometimes under, the village of Sheikh Abd el Gurna. 5km (3 miles) from the river. They are signposted from the Ramesseum.

The Ramesseum

See p107.

On the west bank, at the centre of the Theban necropolis. 5km (3 miles) from the river.

Seti I's Mortuary Temple

If you are unable to see Seti's exquisite reliefs at Abydos (*see opposite & pp84–5*), then you should visit his temple here. Some of the reliefs are best seen from above, so you leap goat-like after the resident guide, from lintel to broken lintel.

On the west bank, at the north end of the Theban necropolis en route to the Valley of the Kings. 4km (2¹/₂ miles) from the river.

Ticket details
See panel on p93 for ticket details.

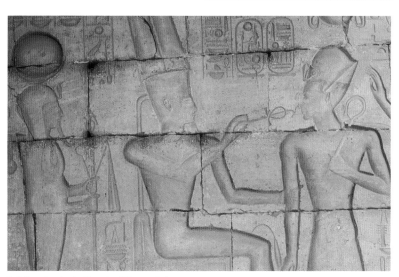

Relief carving in the Temple of Ramses II, Luxor

Valley of the Kings

The Valley of the Kings is an oven of white sand and sun containing 62 tombs, almost all belonging to pharaohs of the 18th, 19th and 20th Dynasties (1570–1090 BC). The tombs were cut into the soft limestone by workmen living at Deir el Medina. Construction and decoration began as soon as a pharaoh came to the throne, and followed a similar pattern in all the tombs. Three corridors lead to an antechamber giving on to a main hall with a sunken floor for receiving the sarcophagus.

The recurrent theme of the decorations has the dead pharaoh, absorbed in the sun god, sailing through the underworld at night in a boat, with enemies and dangers to be avoided along the way. Inscriptions from the *Book of the Dead* provide instructions for charting the course. After this nocturnal voyage the naked body of the sky goddess Nut gives birth each morning to the sun.

Not all tombs have electric lighting (which, in any case, is not very bright), and not all of these are always open. A torch is a useful accessory. Most visitors will be content to see the tombs of Tutankhamun (62), Ramses VI (9), Seti I (17), and Ramses IV (2). Even some of these, unfortunately, may be closed when you visit. For the more energetic, the tomb of Tuthmosis III (34) is well worth the effort.

Tomb 2: Ramses IV (20th Dynasty)

The New Kingdom was already in decline when this tomb was cut. Its decorations are of inferior quality, but the patterns of bright colours against an overall background of white, and the excellent lighting, contribute towards a favourable impression.

The huge pink granite sarcophagus is covered with texts and magical scenes, while Nephthys and Isis on the lid were meant to protect the body – which was, nevertheless, hijacked in antiquity and never found.

Tomb 9: Ramses VI (20th Dynasty)

Originally constructed for Ramses V, this tomb ended after three corridors, but was later extended for Ramses VI, to double its length. The colouring remains fresh throughout. The pillared end-chamber contains fragments of the huge granite sarcophagus of the pharaoh. It is adorned with sunk-relief carvings, which illustrate scenes from religious texts. A magnificent painting of Nut in duplicate adorns its low vaulted ceiling.

Tomb 17: Seti I (19th Dynasty)

At 100m (110yds), the Tomb of Seti I is the longest in the valley. Its reliefs are wonderfully preserved and beautifully executed. On the left wall of the entrance corridor, Seti is greeted by falcon-headed Re-Herakhte, god of the morning sun. The next two corridors are decorated with instructions from the *Book of the Dead* on how to navigate the underworld.

In the three chambers beyond, Seti is shown with various deities. These motifs are then repeated in the second half of the tomb. Finally, there is the burial chamber with astronomical figures on the vaulted ceiling.

Tomb 62: Tutankhamun (18th Dynasty)

This tomb is described on page 106.

THE VALLEY OF THE KINGS

The Valley of the Kings is 7km (4 miles) west of the Nile, along a steeply rising road which curves round the Theban necropolis. The hardy can leave the area by a mountain track starting between Tombs 10 and 16. It divides at the top of the ridge, the left arm descending to Hatshepsut's mortuary temple, the other going on to Deir el Medina.

Valley of the Kings

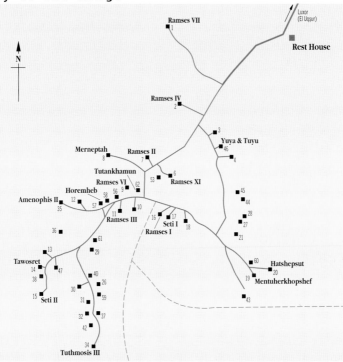

Luxor (El Uqsur)

Rest House

Ramses VII 1

N

Ramses IV 2

3

Yuya & Tuyu 46

4

Merneptah 8   Ramses II 7

Tutankhamun
Ramses VI 62 53 6 Ramses XI
Horemheb 58 56 9
Amenophis II 12 57
35

45
44

28
27

21

11 10
Ramses III 16 17
Seti I 18
Ramses I

36

61

13 29

Tawosret 14 47
38 40 26

30

15 Seti II 31 59

32 37

42

34
Tuthmosis III

60 Hatshepsut 20
19 Mentuherkhopshef

43

VALLEY OF THE QUEENS

This valley contains over 70 tombs of queens, princes and princesses of the 18th, 19th and 20th Dynasties, although only three and sometimes four are open. Unlike the pharaohs, however, these lesser royal figures were not gods, and therefore their tombs are more humble affairs.

Tomb 66: Queen Nefertari (19th Dynasty)

Nefertari was the wife of Ramses II, and is celebrated in stone at Abu Simbel and elsewhere. Her tomb, long closed owing to damage caused by salt deposits, has been marvellously restored and reopened. It is by far the finest in the valley, the wall paintings exquisitely drawn and vividly coloured. Unfortunately, this tomb is usually closed.

Tomb 55: Prince Amun-Her-Khopshef (20th Dynasty)

A smallpox epidemic towards the end of Ramses III's reign killed off several of his sons. In the hall at the bottom of the entrance steps there is a painting showing the pharaoh introducing one of them, Amun-Her-Khopshef, to the gods. The paintings throughout this tomb are fresh and finely executed. At the centre of the burial chamber there is a sarcophagus in human, or rather, mummy, form.

The bones of a six-month-old foetus are displayed in a glass case, and for this very reason, rather than the clarity of the paintings, this tomb seems to hold the attention longer than some of the other tombs.

Tomb 44: Prince Khaemweset (20th Dynasty)

Belonging to another son of Ramses III who fell victim to smallpox, the decorations of this tomb are similar to those of Tomb 55, and are more easily observed, as there is no foetus here to draw the crowds.

Tomb 52: Queen Titi (20th Dynasty)

Although inscriptions describe Titi as a daughter, wife and mother of pharaohs, it is not known to which pharaohs these refer. The paintings are badly faded and damaged. The tomb is arranged like a cross, a corridor leading to a central and three smaller chambers. In the small chamber on the right, Titi is shown with a tree-goddess, and Hathor as a cow. She also appears on the left and right walls of the small chamber ahead.

WORKMEN'S VILLAGE (Deir el Medina)

Deir el Medina means 'monastery of the town', for the workmen's village and the small Ptolemaic temple just north of it were occupied by monks during the early years of Christianity. During the New Kingdom, this was home to skilled artisans who cut and decorated the royal tombs in the Valley of the Kings. The remains of over 70 houses are evident, their mud-brick walls rising on stone foundations along straight and narrow alleys. They had a second storey, or at least a living area on the roof, which was reached by outside stairs. They also fashioned their own tombs, but unlike those of the nobles who decorated their tombs with vivid scenes of everyday life, these workmen more often borrowed motifs from the Valley of the Kings. Over the tomb entrance they would build a man-sized pyramid.

Usually only two or three of these tombs are open. The tomb of Sennedjem (Tomb 1) has a vaulted chamber down steep steps, in which there is a finely painted relief of a funeral feast, and also a nice cameo touch of a cat killing a snake under the sacred tree. The tomb of Peshedu (Tomb 3) shows him praying beneath the tree of regeneration.

On the west bank at the southern end of the Theban necropolis, 4.5km (2³/4 miles) from the river.

One of the many man-sized pyramid tombs at Deir el Medina

Tour: The Theban Necropolis by taxi

Allow four hours to complete this highlight tour of the necropolis. See page 93 for a map of the tour.

Begin at the west bank ticket office. Drive across the cultivation and up through the desert hills into the Valley of the Kings.

1 Tutankhamun's tomb

Discovered by Howard Carter in 1922, this is the only tomb in the Valley of the Kings to have been found with its

Mask of Tutankhamun

contents intact. Owing to the pharaoh's early death at 19 (he had ascended to the throne at the age of 12), the tomb is small and was hurriedly decorated. Its treasures have been removed to Cairo. All that remains here now is the open sarcophagus. Within it lies the outermost of the three gold sarcophagi, and, unseen within that, the mummy of Tutankhamun himself. The right wall shows the coffin transported on a sled. The centre wall shows, from right to left, the opening of the mouth ceremony, Tutankhamun sacrificing to the sky goddess Nut, and the young pharaoh with his *ka* before Osiris. On the left wall is the sun god's boat. The Tomb of Seti I should also be visited. (*For details of this and other tombs in the Valley of the Kings, see pages 102–3.*)

Arrange for your driver to meet you at Deir el Bahri while you walk (or take a donkey) over the path rising out of the Valley of the Kings between tombs 10 and 16. At the top of the ridge, turn left, then descend to Hatshepsut's temple.

2 Hatshepsut's Mortuary Temple (Deir el Bahri)

Apart from Cleopatra, Hatshepsut was the only woman to rule as pharaoh, and she immortalised her reign by brilliantly setting her temple against a pyramid-shaped cliff face to create a powerful yet elegant ensemble (*see pp94–5*).

Immediately south is the village of Sheikh Abd el Gurna, built upon a hillside dotted with nobles' tombs.

3 Tombs of the nobles

Unlike those in the Valley of the Kings, the nobles' tombs are more intimate. (*Others are listed on page 101.*)

Sennufer's tomb

This 18th-Dynasty mayor of Thebes was probably also chief vintner to Amenophis II, and you wonder whether his tomb is not his last laugh on that theme. Vines and grapes are painted on wobbly ceilings, walls and pillars, as though you and Sennufer had had one drink too many.

Ramose's tomb

Ramose was vizier to Amenophis IV, and as you follow these exquisitely carved reliefs around the walls you witness one of the great revolutions in Egyptian history. Begun in classical style, the reliefs continue in the Amarna style, because Amenophis IV had decided to become Akhenaton, and thereafter changed the art and religion of his country.

South from the village is the Ramesseum.

4 Ramesseum

This huge mortuary temple of Ramses II is such a confusing ruin that it is more than sufficient to look at his gigantic fallen statue. Into its mouth Shelley put these ironic words from his poem 'Ozymandias': 'Look on my works, ye Mighty, and despair!'

Alternatively, or additionally, visit Medînet Habu (allowing 30 minutes). Its temple of Ramses III is more complete than the Ramesseum.

Driving south from the Ramesseum and then east, you can pause at the Colossi of Memnon (*see p94*) before continuing over the bridge and back to the east bank.

Fallen head of Ramses II

The Nile Valley: Luxor to Aswân

The Valley of the Nile narrows south of Luxor and the desert impinges more closely on either side. The ribbon of cultivation seems more fragile, its colours more delicate, and the debt that life in Egypt owes to the river becomes more striking. You notice this especially on the east bank beyond Edfu where a narrow strip of palms and cultivation sometimes vanishes altogether.

Like a string of citadels extending Alexandrian power towards Nubia, the Ptolemies built temples along the Nile at Esna, Edfu and Kom Ombo. At Silsileh, 40km (25 miles) south of Edfu, the Nile passes through a defile. Now there are only hills on either side, but there was probably once a cataract.

The bedrock of Egypt changes here from limestone to the harder sandstone that was used in almost all New Kingdom and Ptolemaic temple building. During the reign of Ramses II, the Silsileh quarries were worked by no fewer than 3,000 men for the Ramesseum alone.

Edfu

The present town of Edfu, on the west bank of the Nile (*see p137*), is spread upon the mound of the ancient city of Djeba, which the Ptolemies – who identified the Greek sun god Apollo with Horus – called Apollinopolis Magna. Here Horus avenged the murder of his father Osiris by defeating Seth in titanic combat. To mark this triumph of good over evil, a succession of shrines was built here from earliest dynastic times, culminating with what is the best-preserved ancient monument in Egypt, the Ptolemaic Temple of Horus on the west side of the town.
115km (71 miles) south of Luxor.

TEMPLE FESTIVITIES

As impressive as the ancient temples seem today, they are no more than empty shells, stripped of their furniture, their decoration, their ceremonies and, indeed, their liveliness. But an Edfu text describes how things once were, when the populace of the city could participate in the great festivals that took place at the Temple of Horus: 'Its supplies are more abundant than the sands of the shore. Wine flows in the districts like the inundation pouring from the source of the Nile. Myrrh is on the fire, and incense can be smelt a mile away. It is decorated with faïence, shining with natron, decked with flowers and herbs. The priests and officiants are dressed in fine linen, and the king's party is made fine in its regalia. Its young people are drunk, its populace is happy, its young girls are beautiful to see. Jollity is all around it, carnival is in all its districts, and there is no sleep until dawn.'

Temple of Horus

Until the latter part of the 19th century the temple was almost entirely covered by debris, and houses stood upon its roof. Only its enormous pylon rose clear above the habitations. Even today, the surrounding town obscures your view of it from any distance. And so the impression is all the greater when you arrive at the site and suddenly see the temple all at once. Its enormity is striking, and its near-perfect state of preservation makes it seem like a recent leftover from some epic Hollywood spectacular.

Construction began in 237 BC and continued for 25 years, though some of the decorations were not completed for another 150 years after that. Despite his New Kingdom appearance, the giant pharaoh shown destroying his enemies on the pylon façade is Ptolemy XII Neos Dionysos, who died in 51 BC. He also built at Dendera and was the father of Cleopatra. You pass across a vast colonnaded courtyard towards a pair of huge granite falcon-Horuses, one standing, the other headless and fallen in the dust, which guard the entrance to the temple chambers. These chambers become ever smaller, ever darker, and lead finally to the sanctuary of the god, weirdly illuminated through three small apertures in the ceiling by a dim green light. The reliefs on the inner walls of the sanctuary correspond to those at Dendera, and show a Ptolemaic king entering the sanctuary and worshipping Horus, Hathor and the king's own deified parents. His pendant arms indicate an attitude of reverence.

A sensuously shaped relief of Nut decorates the ceiling of the New Year Chapel which is to the left as you emerge from the sanctuary. Nearby, staircases lead up to the roof, with representations along their walls showing, as at Dendera, how the residing deity was carried up to the roof to be impregnated by the sun. *Western outskirts of Edfu, 2km (1¼ miles) from the Nile. A carriage can be hired at the quay-side. You can walk in 20 minutes from the service taxi depot near the bridge or the train station on the east bank of the river, though private taxis are available from either. Open: daily 6am–6pm in summer; 7am–4pm in winter. Admission charge.*

Pillars inside the Temple of Horus

Esna

Like other towns along the Nile, Esna was, until the end of the 19th century, a port of call for camel caravans crossing the desert from the Sudan (*see p137*). It is still something of a merchant town and weaving centre, with elegant old houses along the west bank of the Nile and in the streets behind. Several of these houses are decorated with fine brickwork and *mashrabiyya* screens. There is also a small and picturesque covered market street, where lengths of fabric are sold or made up into clothing.

Temple of Khnum

Only partly excavated, the Temple of Khnum squats in a pit alongside the covered market street. Here you still have some impression of how many of the ancient monuments appeared until Egyptologists went to work on them in the 19th century, for the rear of the temple remains buried beneath a mound of debris which is partly built over with houses.

Ram-headed Khnum was the patron god of the Cataracts who fashioned

Baubles, bangles and beads

One of the many falcon statues at the temple

man from the mud on his potter's wheel. Ptolemy VI rebuilt the temple in the mid-2nd century BC over the ruins of earlier structures, although almost all that the excavators have laid bare is the hypostyle hall begun two centuries later during the reign of the Roman emperor Claudius.

The roof of the hall is still intact, supported by 24 columns bearing painted capitals in 16 different styles. This is what you come to see, and it is best to stand here, slowly revolving, looking upwards at the myriad palm and composite plant capitals, arranged without order or symmetry, but with the most pleasing effect, as though you were standing among trees, admiring the subtle and powerful architecture of a forest. The last cartouche carved on the temple walls is that of the Roman

emperor Decius, who reigned from AD 249 to 251. He began a series of increasingly severe persecutions against the new Christian religion, and decreed that all its followers must sacrifice to the Roman gods or suffer death.

Testimony to his lack of success in Egypt is to be found in the forecourt of the temple where there are several blocks from an early Christian church, including a lion-headed font carved from an ancient block bearing fine hieroglyphics on the reverse.

Esna is 55km (34 miles) south of Luxor. The Temple of Khnum is at the centre of Esna, a few streets west of the Nile landing stage. It is a 10-minute walk from the service taxi depot; carriages are available from the more distant train station. Open: summer, daily 6am–6.30pm; winter, daily 6am–5.30pm. Admission charge.

The hypostyle hall of the Temple of Khnum

Kom Ombo

The reclaimed land on the east bank around Kom Ombo supports a large Nubian population displaced from their homeland by the rising waters of Lake Nasser. Irrigation keeps the desert at bay, and the fields give rich harvests of wheat and sugar cane. A few kilometres away from the village with its sugar refinery is the Ptolemaic temple.

170km (106 miles) south of Luxor, 45km (28 miles) north of Aswân.

Temple of Sobek and Haroeris

The temple stands on a low promontory overlooking the Nile. Its elevation, its seclusion, and the river flowing by below, make it a magical place to visit, especially from a *felucca* or cruise boat. Its relationship to the landscape reminds you of a Greek

Painted pillar at the Temple of Sobek and Haroeris (Horus)

temple but, though built by Greeks and added to by Romans, the style is pharaonic. As with all Ptolemaic temples, the intention was to reconcile the Egyptian priesthood to foreign rule from Alexandria.

The naos or inner temple was begun by Ptolemy VI Philometor, who built also at Esna, while the hypostyle hall and the pronaos were built by Ptolemy XII Neos Dionysos, whose reliefs adorn the pylon at Edfu. The outer court and the now vanished pylon were added during the time of Emperor Augustus.

This is a symmetrical twin temple, the left side dedicated to falcon-headed Haroeris (Horus in his older aspect), the right side to Sobek, the crocodile god. The two parts of the temple are only physically divided, however, at the two sanctuaries.

You enter the site past a giant ruined gateway, and near it, a small chapel of Hathor. If you wander into the chapel you can see that it is now used as a display room for crocodile mummies dug up from a cemetery close by. The Nile has nibbled away at the temple terrace, causing the pylon to fall, and so you walk directly into the pronaos, its column capitals – some as lilies, some as papyrus – proclaiming the unity of Upper and Lower Egypt. On the interior wall of the façade are fine reliefs depicting various Ptolemaic kings receiving the blessings of Egypt's high gods, and the double crown of the Delta and the Nile Valley.

Some of the striking reliefs at Kom Ombo

In the hypostyle hall beyond, and in the three rising antechambers after that, are more reliefs. One, between the doors into the two sanctuaries, shows Ptolemy Philometor and his sister-wife before Sobek and Haroeris, while Khonsu, son of Amun, inscribes the king's name on a palm stalk, the equivalent of St Peter confirming entry into heaven.

The sanctuaries are badly ruined, but they are all the more revealing for that. Between them, at a lower level, is a crypt which communicates with a chapel to the east. The crypt is now exposed, but was once covered with a sliding slab. It is not difficult, and somewhat eerie, to imagine someone creeping down there from the chapel to make spectral noises at appropriate moments.

An inner corridor passes behind the sanctuaries, and is lined by chapels in

various stages of decoration. Beyond this there is an outer corridor, its walls decorated with Roman reliefs. If you face away from the sanctuaries and look just to the left of centre you will see a relief of the Roman emperor Marcus Aurelius, famous among other things as a Stoic philosopher, but here made to look for all the world like a New Kingdom pharaoh.

To his left are fascinating reliefs of medical instruments, including suction cups, scalpels, retractors, scales, lances, bone saws, chisels for surgery within the skull, and dental tools – testimony to the remarkable degree of medical sophistication in Egypt nearly 2,000 years ago.

4km (2¹/₂ miles) from Kom Ombo village, with its train station and service taxi depot. Cruise boats, however, tie up directly below the temple. Open: daily 8am–8pm. Admission charge.

Rural life

Until the building of the High Dam at Aswân during the 1960s, the Nile annually rose and fell, inundating the surrounding countryside and then withdrawing, leaving behind a rich deposit of mud. There are still some remnants of Egypt's flood-led lifestyle. Villages of mud-brick houses still stand huddled on the low mounds which once kept them clear of the murky waters.

Age-old devices continue to be used to bring water to the fields. The simplest and most ancient of all is the shaduf, a bucket attached to a lever,

operated by hand. The sakiya, introduced in Ptolemaic times, consists of a number of buckets attached to a wheel driven by a circling donkey or ox. Also Ptolemaic is Archimedes' screw, a spiral enclosed within an inclined cylinder which raises water when it is turned.

But the ancient pattern of rural life is changing rapidly. The annual deposits of mud have been replaced by chemical fertilisers, produced by factories operating on the hydroelectric power generated by the High Dam. Harvests have multiplied,

Agriculture remains the basis of the country's economy

The *fellahin* (Egypt's peasantry) depend on farming for their livelihood

but the fields and the river offer fewer nutrients now, and the numbers of birds and fish are diminishing. Even the mud itself has now become an unrenewable resource, and concrete is increasingly being used instead of mud-brick when building houses.

Electricity, however, has brought light to the villages at night – and television, too. The *fellahin*, Egypt's peasantry, are no longer isolated from the wider world. Electric and petrol-driven pumps are replacing the dulling labour of men and animals. By the end of the 20th century, education and primary health care had improved. This ought to have brought brighter prospects. Instead, improved health care has brought a population explosion. *Fellahin* seeking a better existence have been abandoning their diminishing plots in the desperate hope of a better life in the cities, which now hold over half of Egypt's population. Food and jobs are short. The rhythm of the past has been broken, and the future is perilous.

A typical rural settlement by the Nile

Aswân

The layer of sandstone covering Upper Egypt from Edfu southwards is ruptured here by the thrust of underlying granite which the river has sculpted into the rocks and islands of the First Cataract. Throughout history, this is where traffic on the Nile stopped, where cargoes had to be transported round the rocks. Aswân became the entrepôt for the African trade. Although there are things to see, the town's tranquil atmosphere and the beauty of its situation are more conducive to idleness. Fortunately, idleness and sightseeing can be combined by hiring a felucca *and letting the breeze carry you along.*

Aga Khan's Mausoleum

See pp134–5.
On the west bank of the Nile, but closed to the public.

Botanical Garden

See p134.
This botanical island garden, known also as Kitchener's Island, lies between Elephantine Island and the west bank of the Nile and is reached by felucca.
Open: daily 8am–6pm (winter 8am–5pm). Admission charge.

Deir Anba Samaan
(St Simeon's Monastery)

See p135.
On the west bank of the Nile, 2km (1¹/₄ miles) from the river. From the landing stage, you can walk across the sands in about 20 minutes, or hire a camel. Open: daily 9am–5pm (4pm in winter). Admission charge.

Nubian Museum

This delightful modern museum is dedicated to the history and culture of Nubia, and well worth a visit. All the artefacts were found in Nubia, and include a head of King Taharqa, the first Nubian to rule Egypt, and exhibits representing contemporary Nubia.
Tel: (2097) 231911. Open daily 9am– 1pm & 5–9pm (winter 5–8pm).

Elephantine Island

Elephantine is a long palm-covered island opposite Aswân. There is a ferry to the Nubian villages. Otherwise, you can hire a *felucca*, to reach the island's antiquities.

Aswân Museum

Although a lot of the artefacts have been moved to the Nubian Museum, it is worth a look.

Open: Sun–Thur 8am–5pm (6pm in summer), Fri 9am–1pm.
The admission ticket is also valid for Yebu ruins.

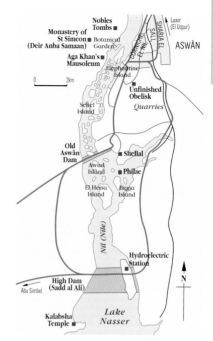

Nilometer

This shaft cut down into the granite bluff on the east side of the island is inscribed with pharaonic, Greek, Latin and Arabic numerals. It was used for measuring the height of the Nile – and therefore the likely harvest, and the tax to be imposed on farmers (*see pp38–9*).

A path from the museum runs 300m (330yds) southeastwards towards a sycamore tree, where you will find the Nilometer. Open: as Aswân Museum. Baksheesh to keeper.

Yebu

Excavations here have revealed the remains of several temples, and also the remains of the homes of the Jewish garrison posted here during the 5th century BC.

Entry to the museum includes admission to the ruins.

Elephantine Island, in the middle of the Nile, sits opposite the modern town of Aswân

The High Dam circuit

It is usual, when visiting the High Dam, to stop – or at least glance at – a few other places of interest along the way. Altogether, the circuit south from Aswân to the unfinished obelisk, then over the old Aswân Dam and back to the east bank via the High Dam, is about 18km (11 miles). Taking a tour or hiring a taxi is the easiest option. Photography at the dams is not permitted, and it is a good idea to bring your passport for identification.

Old Aswân Dam

Built between 1898 and 1902, this dam was part of a vast hydrological project undertaken by the British up and down the length of the Nile, which included barrages at Esna, Nag Hammâdi, and just downriver from Cairo. The height of this dam was twice raised to increase irrigation and hydroelectric output. A road passes over the top of the dam and looks down upon the First Cataract below, though it hardly swirls now.

The unfinished obelisk measures over 27m (88ft)

Aswân High Dam

As the population continued to grow, the old dam could no longer meet Egypt's need for new cultivatable land and increased supplies of electricity. Work began on the High Dam, 6km (3³/4 miles) upstream, in the mid-1960s, and was completed in 1971. Seventeen times as much material went into its construction as was used to build the Great Pyramid of Cheops, and enough metal to build 17 Eiffel Towers. A huge artifical lake, Lake Nasser, reaches back 500km (311 miles) to the Second Cataract in the Sudan. Were the dam to break, a tidal wave would rush down the Nile Valley, inundating most of Egypt's rural and urban population.

Although there are environmental drawbacks, there are also undeniable advantages. The British dam regulated the flow of the Nile during the course of a year; the High Dam can store surplus water over a number of years, balancing low floods against high and ensuring up

The Nile near the Aswân Dam

to three harvests a year. It has already proved its worth. During the 1980s the Nile fell to its lowest levels in 350 years, bringing drought and famine to Ethiopia and the Sudan, but Egypt was spared, and millions of lives saved.

A road passes over the dam, and towards its eastern end there is a viewing platform where you can gain some feeling for the size and controlled energy of the place.

The High Dam can be crossed from 7am to 5pm. There is a toll per person.

Unfinished obelisk

The favoured pink granite found in ancient monuments throughout Egypt and even beyond came from Aswân, much of it from the quarry where you can still see an unfinished obelisk rooted to the bedrock. The work was undertaken during the New Kingdom, and had it been completed, it would have been the largest piece of stone handled in history. Work stopped after

a flaw was discovered in the stone.

The ancient quarry is 2km (1¹/4 miles) south of Aswân. Open: daily 6am–6pm. Admission charge.

Kalabsha Temple

Rebuilt here in the 1970s, this temple's original site was 50km (31 miles) south, in that part of Nubia now beneath the waters of Lake Nasser. It dates from the time of Augustus, and the emperor is shown making offerings to the Egyptian pantheon, for which, in real life, he had the greatest contempt.

At the western end of the High Dam. Open: daily 8am–4pm. Admission charge.

Nobles' tombs

See p134.

The tombs are on the west bank, and can be reached by ferry from the northern end of the Aswân corniche, or by felucca. Open: daily 8am–5pm. Admission charge.

Philae

Completion of the British dam in 1902 submerged the island of Philae for half the year, so that visitors needed to row out upon the river to look at the tops of the temple pylons and columns. In fact, a sense of romance and mystery grew up around the experience. Construction of the High Dam made things worse, however, leaving Philae permanently and almost entirely drowned, so the temples of this historic site were moved.

The decision was taken to transfer the monuments from the old island to another, called Agilqiyyah, which has been moulded to replicate the original. The present site was opened in 1980, and with the growth of vegetation it is impossible to guess that the temples have not been standing here for 2,000 years. Apart from the Vestibule of Nectanebos I, a pharaoh of the 30th Dynasty, the Philae monuments are Ptolemaic and Roman. There are minor temples to Harendotes and Augustus. The three principal monuments, however, are the Kiosk of Trajan, the Temple of Hathor and the Temple of Isis.

The Temple of Hathor

THE CULT OF ISIS

Isis, as wife of Osiris and mother of Horus, increasingly became the focus of worship. The goddess offered an emotive identification so powerful and satisfying that in Ptolemaic times she became identified with all other goddesses of the Mediterranean world, whom she finally absorbed. Isis was the Goddess of Ten Thousand Names. When all else failed, she could still save, and she was worshipped by all. She was the great rival of early Christianity, which may never have given the Virgin Mary prominence but for the Isis cult.

Kiosk of Trajan

On the south side of the island stands this handsome but unfinished building, with 14 great columns bearing beautifully carved floral capitals. Reliefs show Trajan offering incense and wine to Isis, Osiris and Horus. The elegance of the kiosk has made it the characteristic symbol of Philae.

Temple of Hathor

On the east side of the island, this temple was built during the Ptolemaic

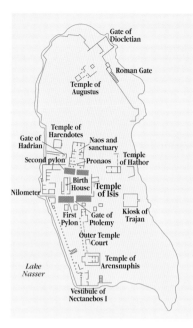

traditional scenes of Ptolemaic kings, attacking the enemy on the First Pylon, on the Second Pylon making offerings to Isis, Horus and Hathor. The walls of the pronaos are likewise covered with scenes of Ptolemaic kings and Roman emperors in pharaonic guise, performing the customary ceremonies.

Later, when this became a church, early Christians added their crosses to the stones. The three antechambers of the naos lead through to the sanctuary with a pedestal on which stood the sacred boat with the image of Isis. On the left wall is a relief of a pharaoh facing Isis, whose wings protectively embrace Osiris. On the right wall, Isis enthroned suckles the infant Horus, while below that she is shown again, suckling a young pharaoh. Here her face was gouged out by Christians.

period, but decorated under Augustus with amusing carvings of music and drinking, for the worship of Hathor was often accompanied by merry-making. The Greeks identified her with the goddess of love, Aphrodite.

Temple of Isis

Two great pylons lead into the temple proper. They are carved with the

PHILAE

Philae, just south of the old Aswân dam, can be reached by taxi and motorboat from Aswân. The island is open daily 7am–6pm. Admission charge. There are nightly **Sound and Light** shows. Check for language schedules first.

The Temple of Isis was moved to a new site because of flooding

Walk: The Aswân Corniche and Bazaar

This walk is less a matter of seeing sights than of sensing the spirit of the place. It is best to begin an hour or so before sunset.

Allow 2 hours. You may want to linger along the way.

Begin on the Corniche el Nil, opposite the northern tip of Elephantine Island, and walk southwards. Follow the numbers shown in green on the map.

1 Corniche el Nil

There is a special fascination in the vista as you walk along the Corniche at Aswân. Instead of the usual placid cultivation, a tidal wave of desert rises on the far bank, islands force the Nile into channels, and boulders break the river's surface like gigantic bathing pachyderms. Although ugly concrete buildings line the landward side of the street, and a hotel looking more like an airport control tower disfigures the northern tip of Elephantine Island, the elemental beauty of the setting remains. The shrine of a Muslim holy man sits on top of the bare hill on the west bank of the Nile, beyond the northern point of Elephantine. The row of small dark openings in the flank of the hill marks the ancient tombs of Aswân's nobles.

Towards the centre of Elephantine Island are Nubian villages, the houses painted pale yellow or brilliant blue. *The road now turns away from the Nile and begins to climb a hill.*

2 Ferial Gardens

On your right, between the road and the Nile, are the Ferial Gardens, standing upon great loaves of granite overlooking the river. Opposite, at the southern tip of Elephantine Island, you can make out the remains of the ancient town of Yebu *(see p117)*. *Across the road from the gardens is a Coptic cathedral.*

3 Coptic Cathedral

Built in 1900 to resemble a domed Coptic church, this was, in fact, the Anglican Church of St Mark, its font a gift of Queen Victoria of England. It has now become a Coptic cathedral, to which visitors are welcome. *Continue south along the road. About 300m (330yds) on, you arrive at the*

*entrance way to the Old Cataract Hotel,
which is on your right.*

4 Old Cataract Hotel

The exterior of this 1902 russet pile
featured in the film of Agatha Christie's
Death on the Nile. If you have timed
your walk well, you will have arrived
here half an hour or so before sunset.
The hotel has a terrace from where,
drink in hand, you can enjoy wonderful
views over the Nile. However, please
note that sometimes non-residents
may not be able to enter the hotel.
(*See Aswân, p172.*)
*When finally the sky has gone through
deepening violets to black, set off back
down the hill as far as the Ferial
Gardens. Instead of going along the
Corniche, however, turn right into*

*Sharia Qasr el Haggag, and then
take the first left into Sharia
el Souk.*

5 Sharia el Souk

This is the main bazaar street of Aswân,
the best bazaar outside Cairo. Sensibly,
in a place which is so burning hot
during the day, it is only now, when the
sun has set, that it becomes thronged
with people.

The first 500m (550yds) of Sharia
el Souk retains something of the
atmosphere of the old caravan days.
Spices, gum, and ebony out of Africa
are traded here, alongside locally woven
rugs and other goods. Buy yourself
some freshly baked flat bread along the
way, and wash it down with pressed
cane juice.

See pp134–5 for orange route

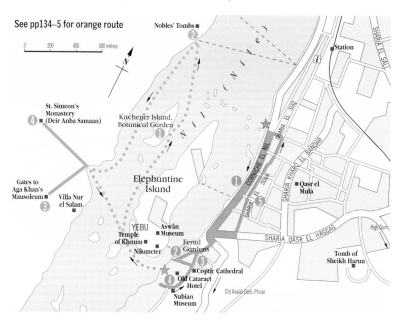

Walk: The Aswân Corniche and Bazaar

Excursion from Aswân

Abu Simbel

Two temples stare out from the cliff face at Abu Simbel. On the left is the Temple of Re-Herakhte with its colossi of Ramses II, and on the right the smaller Temple of Hathor, associated with Ramses' queen, Nefertari. Before the creation of Lake Nasser, the temples overlooked a bend in the Nile and dominated the landscape. As statements of Egyptian might, they served as a warning to any troublesome Nubians on the one hand, while offering a welcome to peaceful traders arriving out of Africa on the other.

Temple of Hathor

The façade is in the form of a buttressed pylon. Between the

Entrance to the pink sandstone temple of Queen Nefertari, wife of Ramses II

ABU SIMBEL

It is 280km (175 miles) south of Aswân, and can be reached by road, but be prepared to join a convoy. There are also flights from Aswân, Luxor and Cairo, and the MS *Prince Abbas* cruises between Lake Nasser and Aswân (*see p162*). Open: 6am–5pm. Admission charge includes local guide.

buttresses are six colossal statues of Ramses and Nefertari. Heads of Hathor adorn the columns of the hypostyle hall inside. On the entrance wall are reliefs of Ramses slaying his enemies, and a very graceful Nefertari with her arms upraised in prayer. Beyond this is the sanctuary with Hathor, as the divine cow, emerging from the rock wall. This, and the façade, suggest the overall symbolism of the temple, which complements that of Re-Herakhte's.

There, Ramses identifies himself with Horus-as-sun-god; here, Nefertari is identified with Hathor, who was wet-nurse and mistress to Horus, as well as wife to the sun god during his day's passage, and mother to his rebirth.

So, in the temple, Hathor emerges as though from the world beyond, where her milk brings life to the souls of the dead; while Nefertari emerges with Ramses into the morning sun.

Temple of Re-Herakhte

Arranged in pairs on either side of the entrance are the four enthroned colossi of Ramses, taller than the Colossi of

Memnon at Thebes, wearing the double crown of Upper and Lower Egypt.

Osiris-type figures of Ramses stand against the piers of the hypostyle hall within. The battle of Kadesh, in which the Egyptians were nearly defeated by the Hittites, is depicted on the left, and Ramses is shown appealing to Amun. On the right, a triumphant Ramses is shown storming a Syrian fortress and capturing Hittites. In the next hall of four pillars Ramses and Nefertari are shown before the boats of Amun and Re-Herakhte. Beyond is the sanctuary, where a divinised Ramses sits with Ptah,

RESCUING THE TEMPLES

Construction of the Aswân High Dam during the 1960s would have meant the drowning of the Abu Simbel temples beneath Lake Nasser. Instead, the UNESCO operation raised them to a new and higher site nearby. As the original temples had been cut into a giant cliff face, an artificial mound had to be constructed, and the temples set into it. A small doorway to the right of Re-Herakhte's temple lets you inside the now air-conditioned dome area.

Amun and Re-Herakhte. The temple progressively depicts Ramses, therefore, as conqueror, hero, and then god.

Excursion from Aswân

The 20m- (66ft-) high colossal figures at the Temple of Re-Herakhte at Abu Simbel

Egypt unearthed

'If you go to Thebes', Josephine is reported to have said to Napoleon, 'do send me a little obelisk.' The imperial capitals of Rome and Constantinople had long ago acquired Egyptian obelisks; and though the British drove Napoleon from Egypt before he could satisfy Josephine's desire, Mohammed Ali made good the growing appetite for Egyptian antiquities by presenting obelisks to Paris, London and New York.

That appetite was stimulated by Napoleon's invasion in 1798, when the scholars accompanying him compiled the famous Description de l'Egypt, the first systematic study of the country, both ancient and modern. It was also during the French occupation that the Rosetta Stone was discovered. Using its parallel Greek text as a key to its ancient Egyptian text, Champollion succeeded in deciphering hieroglyphics in the early 1820s (*see p28*). Now it was possible to read the ancient Egyptians' own descriptions of their lives, their accomplishments and their beliefs.

Scholars such as the Frenchman Auguste Mariette, the German Richard Lepsius, and the Englishman

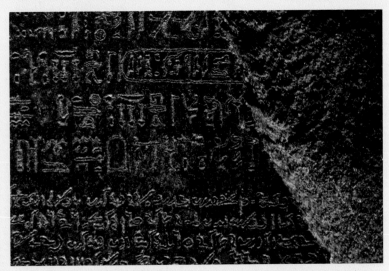

Hieroglyphs (above) and Demotic Egyptian (below) on the Rosetta Stone, now in the British Museum in London

Sir Flinders Petrie laid the foundations for modern Egyptology. Nevertheless, throughout the 19th century, the recovery of information remained secondary to the acquisition of objects. Scholars and adventurers alike freely exported almost anything they discovered – now part of the great collections at the British Museum, the Louvre and elsewhere.

In 1922 all that changed with the discovery of Tutankhamun's tomb by Howard Carter and Lord Carnarvon.

The spectacular find awakened the interest of an increasingly nationalist Egypt in its ancient heritage. The old rule of finders-keepers was challenged, and instead of being taken abroad, the treasures were put on display in Cairo. The modern spirit is expressed by the UNESCO inscription at Abu Simbel: 'These monuments do not belong solely to the countries who hold them in trust. The whole world has the right to see them endure'.

Cartouche enclosing the name of Ramses II at his temple in Abu Simbel

Getting away from it all

'Perhaps the most wonderful part of desert life is the desert night', wrote the Egyptian explorer Ahmed Hassanein early this century. 'It is as though a man were deeply in love with a very fascinating but cruel woman. She treats him badly, and the world crumples in his hand; at night she smiles on him and the whole world is paradise.'

DESERT DRIVING AND CAMEL TREKKING

Paradise can in fact be approached by public transport, which follows paved roads to all the oases of the Western Desert but hiring a vehicle will give you greater freedom to explore.

Some roads in remote areas, such as those between the oases of Bahariya and Farafra, and particularly between Farafra and Dakhla, can get badly potholed and sandswept, but provided your car has been well maintained, a

two-wheel drive vehicle should be entirely adequate for on-road driving anywhere in Egypt. Take sensible precautions, such as taking plenty of water and petrol, travelling in pairs in remoter areas, and avoiding night driving over dodgy roads.

Off the beaten track

As soon as you get off the road, however, even just to camp overnight in the desert, you must have a four-wheel drive vehicle. Fortunately, you can sleep

Nomadic inhabitants of the White Desert

out beneath the stars in the must-see **White Desert**, 50km (31 miles) north of Farafra. White chalk formations are nightly licked into abstract sculptures by the windblown sand, and everything, both desert and sleepers alike, awakens glistening in the morning as though freshly whitewashed.

Arrange things locally with Saad, of Badawiya Hotel in Farafra town. For cost of overnight trips into the White Desert in a six-person jeep, call mobile: 012 2148343 or (202) 05758076. www.badawiya.com

Turquoise mines

In Sinai, one of the best off-road adventures is to the **Wadi Magara turquoise mines**, which are reached by following an ancient track eastwards up Wadi Sidri from Abu Rudeis, midway down the west coast of the peninsula. At 25km ($15^1/_2$ miles) Wadi Magara opens off to the north and it is then a short distance to the mines. They are round the final leftwards bend, 40m (130ft) above the valley floor on the left. The mines were worked as early as the First Dynasty, and as you walk deep into the valley wall you sometimes notice small turquoises. If you climb higher you come to carvings on the rock face depicting 4th- and 5th-Dynasty pharaohs. Directly across the valley, on the hill opposite, are the remains of workshops, workers' houses, and a fort, all pharaonic. Back down on the sandy wadi floor you can picnic beneath the shade of an acacia tree.

At the eastern end of Wadi Sidri, head north 50km (31 miles) to the larger turquoise mines of **Serabit el Khadim**, where there is also a 12th-Dynasty sanctuary to Hathor. If you turn south at the end of Wadi Sidri, you will enter, almost immediately, the broad **Wadi Moqattab**, the Valley of Inscriptions. Here you will find mostly Nabataean and Greek, but also Coptic and Arabic texts, dating from between the 1st and 6th centuries AD.

In Cairo you can arrange jeep safaris into the Western Desert or to Sinai through Ahmed Moussa, Pan Arab Tours. Tel: (202) 6905240. Check www.desertlodge.net or www.panarabtours.com

Camels

You can also venture into the wadis of Sinai, and trek over the mountains, on camelback. Camels with guides can be hired at Dahab, Nuweiba, Sharm el Sheikh and St Catherine's.

Treks usually take from one to ten days. Be prepared to produce a medical certificate, and have your own sleeping bag and first aid kit. You may be required to register your trip with the police for security purposes.

'The noses, ears, mouths and eyes of our party carried away enough of Egypt, which had been held suspended in the air, to found an oasis in the desert.'
William Jarvie
Letters Home from Egypt and Palestine, 1903–4, New York, 1904

The desert

Egypt has three deserts. Sinai and the Eastern Desert are both, for the most part, broken, mountainous areas with some vegetation in the shelter of their deeply indented valleys. Bedouin (nomadic Arab herdsmen) inhabit both these regions. The Western Desert, an extension of the Sahara, is entirely different. Among the hottest and driest places in the world, it is a level plateau utterly without water or vegetation except where occasional springs surface at deep depressions to create oases. White sands, formed by the disintegrating rock strata, move in graceful, undulating dunes of awesome power, encroaching on fields and villages, submerging telephone poles and engulfing entire trucks. The mighty army of the 6th-century BC Persian king Cambyses was swallowed by the sands during an expedition to Siwa, and in 1805, a 2,000-strong camel caravan disappeared into the same sands.

The living desert

Animal life is dependent on vegetation, and so only the most specialised of species can inhabit the deserts. Even these are found mostly near oases or in the northern scrubland along the Mediterranean coast. Deser mammals include the gazelle, desert fox, hyena, jackal and gerbil. Migratory birds such as swallows, hoopoes, wagtails and warblers pause in the oases during their flights, attracted by the abundant insect life. Snakes and lizards are more permanent residents; indeed the Egyptian cobra, *Naja haje*, is almost an ancient monument, having served so strikingly as the uraeus on pharaonic crowns.

Steps and arch on an old path through the rocks

Sunrise from the summit of Mount Sinai

The animal perhaps most associated with the desert is the camel. Introduced from Asia, it became plentiful only during the Ptolemaic period. The ones you now see in Egypt are bred mostly in Sudan. They are driven along the Darb el Arbain, the Forty Days' Road, from Darfur to the Tuesday-morning camel market (souk el Gamal) at Daraw, 6km (3³/₄ miles) south of Kom Ombo. Others continue by train to the Friday-morning camel market at Birqosh, 35km (22 miles) northwest of Cairo.

Feluccas

If you have not already sailed in a felucca, you will almost certainly do so in Aswân when you visit the islands in the Nile and the sites on the west bank (see pp134–5). You will rapidly discover that you have become addicted to its pleasure, and the only cure is to indulge in some more.

Excursion to Sehel

You could start with the half-day journey from Aswân to the island of Sehel and back. Though the current is against you as you head upstream, your boatman extends the gaff upwards, giving great height and grace to the sail, which then fills with the prevailing wind.

From the island there is a view of the rocks and swirling waters of the First Cataract, although the Nile hardly pounds and foams as once it did, before the building of the British dam. On the other hand, the ferocity of the sun as you step ashore should warn you how dangerous its rays really are, cool though you may feel as you sail along the river.

With its head into the wind, but taking advantage of the current, your *felucca* tacks back down the Nile. If you drink from the river, it is said, you will return to Egypt. You might have thought you would drop dead instead. In fact, the Nile has a fresh and somewhat organic taste, and the boatmen drink from it all the time,

TOURS

Agencies along the corniche at Aswân and Luxor may put together a party of six to eight people for a boat, though you are free to do that yourself. You can also decide on a shorter journey, overnight from Aswân to Kom Ombo, for example, if you are pressed for time. Find out the official rate first from the tourist office; the actual price that you finally agree with the *felucca* captain will depend on season (cheaper in summer) and demand. Payment should be made only at the end of the trip. As an easier option, several adventure tour operators offer a *felucca* trip as part of their Egypt packages.

saying there is no bilharzia above Esna, and certainly no danger of it from fast-flowing water. On the other hand, they say tourists actually get upset stomachs from drinking ice-cold bottled water and soft drinks.

Drop out for five days

The longer *felucca* journey between Aswân and Luxor requires some forethought and preparation. Do check the security situation with the tourist police first. For one thing there is the choice of blowing upstream with the wind from Luxor to Aswân, or floating downstream from Aswân to Luxor on the current. The latter is more predictable, and it can also be a bit cheaper, costing about LE100 per person aboard a six- to eight-passenger vessel. Stops are made at Kom Ombo, Edfu and Esna but, generally, *feluccas* only go as far as Edfu. Food might be included, and a blanket, and there is no night sailing. For an extra sum, the captain, usually an English-speaking Nubian, will also provide food, though it would probably be a good idea if you

supplemented this with your own supplies. Unless you are willing to drink from the Nile like the boatmen, also take along three litres of bottled water for each day of the journey. You will be sleeping either on planking aboard the *felucca*, or on the ground ashore. Nights can be chilly throughout most of the year, and downright cold during winter, so you will need warm blankets or a sleeping bag. Also keep a sweater for the evenings, insect repellent, and, remembering how misleading the feel of the breeze can be, some form of protection – sunscreen lotion, hat, etc – against the sun, which is all the more intense for being reflected off the water.

Feluccas moored outside the Old Cataract Hotel at Aswân

Tour: *Feluccas* and camels

From tropical gardens to desert sands on the West Bank, this journey of unusual variety near Aswân combines a taste of adventure with abundant moments of sheer delight.

Allow 4 hours.

Begin by hiring a felucca *below the terrace of the Old Cataract Hotel or along the Corniche el Nil (see map on p123, following the numbers in orange).*

1 Botanical Garden

Look out for egrets and hoopoes wading among the rocks as you sail round the southern point of Elephantine Island. General Kitchener became Consul-General in Egypt in 1911, and this island was presented to him then. Here he indulged his passion for flowers, ordering plants from around the world. Now known as the Botanical Garden, it is pleasant to walk along its shady paths, enjoying its fragrances and the colourful birds (*see p116*).
Sail northwards to the bare hill on the west bank of the Nile.

2 Nobles' tombs

A trek up a sandy path from the landing stage brings you to a line of tombs cut into the cliff face (*see p119*). They all date from the late Old Kingdom to the early Middle Kingdom and belonged to the governors, princes and priests whose lives revolved around the control of the Nubian trade. The most interesting is the tomb of Sirenput II (Tomb 31), who was a governor of Aswân during the Middle Kingdom. An undecorated pillared hall leads, by way of a corridor lined with Osiris statues, to a smaller hall, its pillars and walls covered with paintings of Sirenput and his family. On the rear wall, Sirenput sits at a table, his son before him clutching flowers, while all around are wonderfully coloured hieroglyphics.
You now sail southwards to a cove where a path leads up to the gates of Aga Khan's Mausoleum. Unfortunately, the Mausoleum is not open to the public.

3 Aga Khan's Mausoleum

Aga Khan III lived at the white villa here, and was buried in the domed mausoleum just above it in 1957. His fine white Carrara marble tomb was carved in Cairo with geometric patterns and Quranic inscriptions. His wife, the Begum, lies buried next to him.

Aga Khan III was spiritual leader of the Ismailis, a Shi'ite sect, and also a man of considerable wealth and weight. At his diamond jubilee in 1945 he was weighed against diamonds which were then distributed among his followers. His playboy son, Ali, predeceased him, and he was succeeded by his more earnest grandson Karim, Aga Khan IV. *Near the* felucca *landing you can hire a camel for an accompanied ride to St Simeon's. Alternatively, you can walk across the soft sand in 20 minutes. The Mausoleum is closed to the public.*

4 St Simeon's Monastery (Deir Anba Samaan)

Fields and gardens once filled the desert valley leading from the Nile up to the monastery. That was until 1173, when the monks were driven out and their monastery ruined by Saladin who feared it might be used as a refuge for Christian Nubians during their forays into Egypt.

Built like a fortress in the 7th century, enough survives within St Simeon's 10m- (33ft-) high walls to create an evocative impression of the community which once flourished here. There is a roofless basilica with badly damaged paintings of Christ and various saints in its apses. Nearby rises a three-storey keep, off which were the living quarters, including a refectory, cells for 300 resident monks, and dormitories for hundreds more pilgrims, as well as bakeries and workshops (*see p116*).
Return to your felucca *to sail back to Aswân.*

For practical information on the sights see pp116–19. Also, refer to the map on p123.

The Old Cataract Hotel was used as a backdrop for the film of Agatha Christie's *Death on the Nile*

Cruise: The Nile

To see Egypt from the deck of a cruise boat is one of the most pleasurable experiences of a lifetime. These days, cruises are mainly between Luxor and Aswân, and generally last from three to five days. For a longer cruise, a sail to Dendera and Abydos to the north of Luxor is possible.

Cruises can be in either direction, but the typical route described here is from Luxor north to Dendera and Abydos, and then south, passing Luxor, to Esna, Edfu, Kom Ombo and Aswân. If your cruise begins at Aswân, follow this summary in reverse.

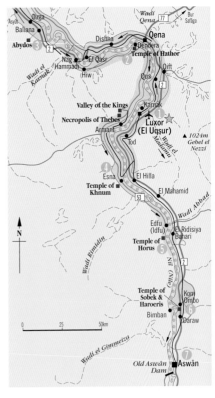

1 Luxor

Board mid-afternoon. The following day take in the Temple of Luxor and Karnak on the east bank of the Nile, and the Theban necropolis on the west bank (*see pp92–107*). Sail north at evening, tying up at Dendera overnight.

2 Dendera

Buses are on hand for your visit to the Ptolemaic Temple of Hathor at Dendera (*see pp86–7*). The 1km (²/₃-mile) walk along a country road leading straight to the temple is cool and beautiful, especially if it is early in the morning.

3 Abydos

Your boat may pass through the Nag Hammâdi barrage and under the railway bridge (so close a squeeze that the upper deck is cleared), to tie up off

The romantic Nile cruise was invented by Thomas Cook

Abydos, but usually the boat will remain at Dendera while buses transfer you to Abydos, and the temple built by Seti I (*see pp84–5*). You then return to Dendera by bus, and sail southwards past Luxor, tying up overnight at Esna.

4 Esna

At Esna there is a barrage, built by the British in 1906–7, which serves also as a bridge. There is a newer lock, through which your boat must pass, but delays can still occur if too many boats wish to pass at the same time. This may happens while you are asleep, or in the morning hours while you are visiting the Ptolemaic Temple of Khnum (*see pp110–11*).

5 Edfu

About midday you arrive at Edfu where you are met by carriages which take you to the huge Ptolemaic Temple of Horus (*see p109*). Later in the day you sail south to Kom Ombo. Beyond Edfu the landscape changes, with the desert sometimes spilling down to the east bank of the Nile.

6 Kom Ombo

This double Temple of Sobek and Haroeris (Horus), also dating from the Ptolemaic period, enjoys a lovely setting on a low promontory overlooking the river (*see pp112–13*). You tie up beneath it and possibly spend the night here, sailing for Aswân in the morning.

The ribbon of cultivation on either side of the river is very thin now, and often the desert presses in on both sides. South of Kom Ombo much of the local population speaks the Nubian language, and it gives you the feeling that you are entering another world.

7 Aswân

You arrive in Aswân at midday (*see pp116–25*). It feels like sailing into an oasis. The town stands brightly on the east bank, and a great wave of desert rises on the west. Islands, *feluccas* and granite outcrops seem to fill the Nile. There is something restful yet exciting about this place, as if you have finally reached the tropics.

The cost of the cruise includes visits to the sites en route. See pp162–3 for details.

Monasteries

Throughout their long history, Egypt's monasteries have been designed for getting away from it all. It was not to escape Roman persecution that early Christians fled to the deserts, rather to escape the fleshpots of the Nile. To stay overnight at a Coptic monastery is not exactly fun, but it is certainly an escape from modern living.

A pilgrim's account dating from the late 4th century describes Wadi Natrûn, known also as Scete: 'The place called Scete is set in a vast desert, and the way to it is to be found or shown by no track and no landmarks of earth, but one journeys by the signs and courses of the stars. Water is hard to find. Here are men made perfect in holiness, for so terrible a spot could be endured by none save those of austere resolve and supreme constancy'.

Demons and fables

If this is not enough to challenge you, consider the demons you can rid your-self of. At the Monastery of Baramus the monks exhibit a shirt emblazoned with blood, its splatterings in the shape of numerous crosses. They tell you that not long ago a troubled man came to the monastery. On approaching the altar of God he shrank back in horror, and in a strange voice, he cursed the monks, who anointed him with oil on his wrists and head. This caused the devil to erupt from his body, splattering the shirt with blood as he went.

It is wonderful to be a child and to be told incredible bedtime stories. It is even more wonderful to be an adult and to sit beneath a vine trellis sipping tea within ancient walls somewhere in the darkening Western Desert, and to hear the incredible related from the lips of a bearded monk in a long black robe with a starry cowl pulled over his head. You are then shown to your quarters and advised to get to sleep early.

The hermits

Baramus may well be the world's oldest, indeed the world's first, monastery. It is surrounded by hermits' caves for those who find even monastic life too cosy; and as you lie in bed you think of them, alone in the Western Desert, practising humility through speaking to scorpions.

One such hermit was disturbed by bursting shells and a rain of shrapnel: the Battle of El Alamein was exploding around him. A startled soldier, seeing him emerge from his cave, nearly shot him dead. Even then the hermit would not move, declaring that the war was a devilish scheme to interrupt his prayers. When the smoke cleared, the British HQ in Cairo sent its apologies for the inconvenience caused.

A section for sinners

At 4am you are wakened by the sound of bells ringing through the desert air. You join the silent flow of robed figures who sweep across the moonlit courtyard of the monastery towards the ancient church. Here, amid dim candles and medieval icons, the day begins with two hours of chanting followed by three hours of liturgy in discordant Coptic and Arabic, enlivened

occasionally by the tinkle of triangles. Visitors are normally left at the outermost end of the nave, in the section reserved for sinners, where you can sleep through much of the chanting, and even creep away altogether. For the monks, however, their devotions are followed by an eight-hour day in the surrounding fields.

In case you arrived at Baramus looking for fun, there is a notice announcing that 'Looking at the wilderness kills the lusts of the soul. Visiting the monastery should be considered a trip of rebuke and not one for pleasure.'

See p178 for information on visiting Coptic monasteries.

The Coptic Monastery of St Paul (Deir Anba Bula), south of St Antony's (Deir Anba Antunius)

Oases

To the ancient Egyptians the oases were gifts not of the Nile but of the sky. In fact, the four inner oases of the Western Desert mark the line of a prehistoric branch of the Nile, and to this day feed from ancient stores of underground water.

The ancients were not entirely wrong about the sky's role in creating the oases. *Wahat* (cauldron) was the pharaonic name for the depressions in which the oases sit. Eroded by winds in the course of millennia, the depressions dipped down towards the water table while atmospheric pressure caused the natural springs to bubble to the surface.

And so, as you pick your way along the hot, thin line of asphalt through a landscape of lethal immensity, you can imagine that these islands of fertility owe as much to the sky forces above as to the hidden waters below.

The western loop

A road over 1,000km (620 miles) in length loops far out into the Western Desert from Gîza, at first southwest to **Baharîya** and **Farafra** oases, continuing southeast to **Dakhla Oasis,** and then due east to **El Khârga Oasis,** before finally turning northeast to join the Valley of the Nile near Asyût. A road links El Khârga with Luxor, opening up

the entire New Valley (as the governorate containing the four inner oases, but not distant Siwa, is called) to the large-scale tourism already attracted to Upper Egypt.

The oases are fascinating microcosms of Egyptian rural life and history, and they can serve as bases for short trips into the surrounding desert wilderness. You can explore one or two of them in a long weekend, or see them all in the course of a week's journey.

Baharîya and Farafra are the most inaccessible of the oases, and so best preserve their traditional feel. The native architecture is particularly handsome at Farafra, from where also you can visit the White Desert (*see p129*). Dakhla is probably the best single oasis to visit.

Date palms and gardens

The lush gardens and date groves of **Dakhla Oasis** strike a pleasing contrast with the surrounding pink and ochre rocks of the desert. It has large reserves of water, though much of it is brackish, and over 700 springs. At **Mut Talata**, 3km (1³/₄ miles) west of Dakhla's capital town of Mut, you will find a hot sulphur pool. Muddy brown and smelly, its effect on aching muscles is wonderful and you will soon forget the aroma of rotten eggs. The best time to go is at night, when a layer of steam drifts across its surface and the sky is full of stars.

There is a lovely freshwater spring at **Bir el Gebel**, 35km (22 miles) west of Mut, and a 5km (3-mile) detour off the main road to El Qasr. Here you can feel that you are getting away even from the oasis. A few palm trees sprout beside the pool which is at the foot of Dakhla's 400m (1,300ft) northern escarpment. From the top there is a marvellous view. In one direction are the villages of the oasis. In the other, below the escarpment, is a field of boulders smoothed into parallel, identical teardrops by the wind.

The old part of **El Qasr**, 40km (25 miles) north of Mut, is an all but abandoned fortress town of towers and domes rising from a hill, though when you are in it you seem to be underground. Its alleys were covered for shade and built low and narrow to force any invaders to dismount, making them vulnerable to ambush within the maze of passages and dead ends. The thick-walled houses jut with wooden beams. The door lintels of many are single blocks of beautiful dark wood, engraved with Quranic verses. You can fully explore two of the houses which have been renovated by the Egyptian Antiquities Organisation.

Brides used to take a ritual bath in Cleopatra's Spring, one of the many springs at Siwa Oasis

Red Sea resorts

The Red Sea resorts are now among the most popular of Egypt's destinations. Some resort hotels have spectacular surroundings and can be elegant and relaxing. After an early burst of development, an effort has recently been made to ensure the landscape blends in with the environment.

On the western shores of the Red Sea lie the resorts of **Hurghada**, **El Gouna**, **Makadi Bay** and **Soma Bay**. All are within 75 minutes of Hurghada airport and are set against the backdrop of desert sands. Water sports and diving are the principal activities in these resorts; the beautiful coral reefs of this region can also be viewed from the comfort of a glass-bottomed boat. There is a championship golf course at the purpose-built resort centre of Soma Bay, and horse riding and go-karting are on offer at El Gouna.

Away from the sporting activities, Hurghada offers a reasonable choice of shops, including a bazaar, while El Gouna – built on islands amid lagoons – also boasts a range of shops, lively bars and restaurants, as well as a traditional market, Souk el Balad. Its museum includes an observatory and aquarium. Further north, on the Sinai peninsula, is **Sharm el Sheikh**, comprising a number of resort areas. These range from the modern amenities of **Na'ama Bay** to the traditional lifestyle of **Sharm el Maya** with its natural harbour and Arab bazaars. Established holiday centres, they offer camel treks, good swimming and excellent water-sports facilities (*see also p81*).

Venturing away from the water, visitors can enjoy trips to Mount Sinai, to St Catherine's, the fourth-century monastery at its foot (*see p80*), or to the spectacular surroundings of the rocky Coloured Canyon.

At the southern end of the Red Sea Riviera is **Marsa Alam**. Less developed than many of the other resorts, this offers good-quality coral reefs, rocky coves and a tranquil environment.

The best of diving

From the western shore of the Red Sea, sites such as **Abu Nahas Reef** are easily accessible. This 'ships' graveyard' provides good wreck diving, and reef fish, lion fish and octopus are among the species that can be seen amid the coral here. **Siyul Kabirah**, around the island of Big Siyul, has black coral and caves, and **Sha'ab Abu Ramada** – known as the 'Aquarium' – boasts a vast range of reef fish.

The best stretch of coastline, both for divers and for the rest, is from **Ras Muhammad** at the southern tip of Sinai to **Taba**, 1km (²/₃ mile) from the Israeli border. This area is the **Gulf of Aqaba**, a northern extension of the Red Sea, rivalled only by Australia's Great Barrier Reef for dive sites. Its resorts are readily accessible, its sharks well fed enough to have no interest in eating you, and its landscape beautiful. Ras Muhammad is an undeveloped nature reserve reached only by private vehicle or boat from Sharm el Sheikh. Despite the fact that there are no camping facilities, it is still crowded at weekends.

From Marsa Alam divers can head out to the Elphinstone Reef and the Samadai Reef. Here, sheer walls plunge 70m (230ft) down into crystal-clear waters, and hammerhead sharks, tuna, spinner dolphins and barracuda are among the creatures to be seen.

Taba

Ever since the Israelis handed Taba to the Egyptians in 1989, new hotels and resorts have sprung up along the coast to Sharm el Sheikh. The diving here and off Pharaoh's Island is interesting. When Saladin captured the island from the Crusaders in 1170 he built the fortress, now restored, that you see on it today. (*See also pp76–7 and pp160–61.*)

Sandy beaches line the clear waters of the Red Sea

Shopping

Simply to list Egypt's traditional crafts and wares brings to life the sights and scents of the bazaar: spices and perfumes, brass and copperware, gold and silver jewellery, glass, ceramics and precious stones, carpets, inlay work and mashrabiyya, *cottons and leatherwork. Places like Cairo's Khan el Khalili and Aswân's Sharia el Souk are a browser's and shopper's dream. There is also the chance to buy antiquities at reputable shops both in Upper Egypt and in Cairo, and antiques from different periods at Alexandria's Rue Attarine.*

The country is, however, also moving with the times, and a new generation of craftsmen and designers is translating Egyptian themes into stylish and competitively priced clothing, jewellery, furnishings, household items and so on, with an eye to international appeal. You will soon discover that shopping in Egypt is one of the best ways of getting to know the country.

Fixed-price department stores and most shops will display prices. The shops in the arcades of major hotels and shopping malls will mark prices in Western numerals; in local shops and department stores, prices are given in Arabic numerals, which is a good reason to become familiar with them (*see p29*).

Bargaining at bazaars

You will discover that time is cheap in the bazaars of Egypt – cheap for Egyptians, if not for you. If you want to bargain well, you must be prepared to dedicate some time to it. A stallkeeper will always ask more than he expects to get. The traditional response is to offer half as much. After several minutes, perhaps half an hour, a price midway between the extremes is agreed. That is the traditional way.

The virtue of a bazaar is that there is plenty of competition, and so, by shopping around, you ought to get a feel for price and be able to strike a good bargain. In Cairo's Khan el Khalili, for instance, you will find all the copperware in one area, all the spices in another, all the wood and mother-of-pearl inlay in yet another. This allows you to compare styles, quality and price. It can be a good idea, also, to go to a fixed-price shop first – at least you will know the price you are out to beat.

It helps when bargaining if you appear dispassionate. The more that you show your interest, the more the seller is likely to make you pay for it.

A good technique is to bargain first over something you do not want, and then casually to start bargaining over what you do want, almost as though you did not want anything and just bargained for the sport of it.

It is, in fact, a sport, and there are rules as well as tricks of the game. Your first extreme counter-offer will be laughed at and you may feel silly. Do not worry; that is only part of the game. If you feel that after several rounds of offers and counter-offers you are getting nowhere, walk out. The vendor will stop you if he thinks there is still a deal to be made. You can always go elsewhere.

The essence of a bargain, of course, is not to arrive at some preconceived fraction of the original asking price, but to feel that you have paid a price you could not have bettered elsewhere. It is a mark of your bargaining skills.

What to buy
Alabaster
Vases, statuettes and reproduction antiques such as scarabs are often carved from alabaster. The best place to shop is in Luxor, or workshops in the village of Gurna amid the Theban necropolis. All too frequently you will be pestered by touts offering you alabaster 'antiquities'; if you want one, offer only a tenth of the asking price.

Antiquities
Any antiquities offered to you on the street are bound to be fake, which is not to say there are no genuine pharaonic, Coptic and Islamic artefacts around, although they are somewhat overpriced. However, it is illegal to export genuine antiquities.

Books and prints
Books on Egypt and Egyptology, as well as facsimile prints of the work of such 19th-century artists as David Roberts, are available in large bookshops in major tourist centres throughout the country. Cairo, however, is the place to look for originals of rare books and prints.

Brass and copper
Brass and copper work has long been a Cairo tradition, and the standard is still high today. The finest items are the big brass trays which can serve as table tops, and for which wooden stands are available. More portable items include candlesticks, lamps, mugs and pitchers, though be sure that anything you intend to drink out of is coated on the inside with another metal, such as silver, as brass or copper can be highly poisonous in contact with some substances.

Camels
Most probably you will just want to browse and not buy at the Souk el Gamel in Cairo (particularly lively early Friday morning), or Daraw, near Kom Ombo in Upper Egypt, where the camels are brought for sale after being herded up from Sudan. The bargaining and trading are fascinating to watch.

Clothing and fabrics

The *galabiyya*, the full-length traditional garment of Egyptian men, is popular with both male and female visitors as comfortable casual wear. Fancier versions can also serve as evening wear for women. There are three basic styles: the *baladi* or peasant style, with wide sleeves and a low rounded neckline; the *saudi* style, more form-fitting, with a high-buttoned neck and cuffed sleeves; and the *efrangi* or foreign style, a floor-length shirt with collar and cuffs. A more recent phenomenon is designer fashion with international appeal.

Egyptian cotton is the finest in the world, which is another good reason for buying Egyptian clothing, or having it made up for you. If you do, be warned that the workmanship is not always up to scratch.

Glass

Muski glass, usually turquoise or dark brown and recognisable by its numerous air bubbles, has been handblown in Cairo for centuries. It is now turned out as ashtrays, candlesticks and glasses.

Jewellery

Egyptian jewellery mostly mimics the more obvious pharaonic motifs such as the scarab (for good luck), cartouche, the *ankh* (the symbol of life) and the Eye of Horus.

Items of Islamic motif show little popular imagination, the designs being usually confined to hands and eyes for warding off evil or bearing inscriptions of 'Allah'. Anything outside these two motifs is usually perceived as bad taste. The exceptions are simple turquoise strands and Bedouin silverwork.

Leatherwork, shoes and accessories

The most common items on offer are handbags, belts, suitcases and hassocks, although Egyptian leather is not of the best quality. Also, more interesting than comfortable are camel saddles. Shoes are possibly the major fashion retail item, and range from the highly stylish to cheap and practical. They do not wear as well as Western-made shoes, but the oriental leather slippers are a good buy.

Musical instruments

Cairo is a good place to buy traditional musical instruments. These include the *oud* (lute), the *rabab* (viol), the *nai* (flute), the *kanoon* (dulcimer), the *tabla* (drum), the *mismare baladi* (oboe) and the *duf* and *riq* (forms of tambourine).

Nargiles

You often see men smoking the *nargile* or 'hubble-bubble' pipe at cafés. A moist lump of scented tobacco (*shisha*) is put into a small terracotta cup and is kept alight by a piece of glowing charcoal. By sucking on a flexible tube, the smoke is drawn down the stem of the pipe through a container of water which reduces tar and makes for a very mild smoke. The best pipes will have glass rather than brass bodies for holding the water.

Papyrus

The sheets of 'papyrus' sold with pharaonic scenes painted on them are often made from banana leaves. Real papyrus can withstand being crumpled up; if the one you are offered cracks when you crumple it, do not buy it. You can see genuine papyrus being made at Dr Ragab's Papyrus Institute in Cairo (*see p149*), and at Luxor near the museum, where you can also buy it.

Scents and spices

For a thousand years, Cairo has been one of the world's greatest centres for the trade in spices, which also explains its position as a purveyor of perfume essences.

Egypt provides essences to French perfumiers who, apart from combining them in their own inimitable way, also dilute them in nostril-blasting alcohol. Egyptian perfume, on the other hand, is often made by diluting the essence in oil. Scents, spices and herbs for cooking and cures are also sold in Khan el Khalili, as well as in Aswân's souk.

Weavings, carpets, tents and tapestries

Egypt is not particularly renowned for its carpets, but Aswân is the best place to look around for small carpets and weavings of all sorts, which originate in neigbouring regions. Tent-making, on the other hand, is a Cairene speciality, and you will often see beautiful appliqué tents used in street festivals. You don't have to buy a whole tent: they are made in sections, and you can buy a piece as a cushion cover.

Rural motifs and bold colours give the world-famous tapestries of Harraniyya, a village near Gîza, their naive charm. They are the creations of children who are taught traditional crafts at the Wissa Wassef Art School, which makes for an interesting visit.

Woodwork and inlay

Cairene craftsmen are known for their wooden trays, game boards and boxes intricately inlaid with mother-of-pearl and coloured bits of wood which are surprisingly cheap. *Mashrabiyyas*, those wonderfully carved wooden screens found in old Cairene houses, occasionally appear in the bazaars where they can often fetch a fairly high price.

'Hubble-bubble' pipes make an unusual gift

Where to buy

Almost everything you might want to buy is available in Cairo, in some cases only in Cairo. Certain places may have their special attractions, the souk in Aswân for example, or the Rue Attarine flea market in Alexandria, but you cannot beat Cairo for its range of stores and boutiques, and for its labyrinthine Khan el Khalili, with its exotic medieval atmosphere.

In Upper Egypt and at the Red Sea resorts, a range of reputable jewellers, clothiers and the like will be found in the shopping arcades of major hotels, but here, and in Alexandria, there are no shops worth singling out. Just stick to the hotels, or head towards the market.

CAIRO
Antiquities
Ahmed Dahba
5 Sikket el Badestan, in the heart of Khan el Khalili.

Books and prints
American University in Cairo (AUC) Bookstore
In Hill House on the university campus, 113 Sharia Qasr el Aini, near Midan el Tahrir.
Tel: (202) 7942964.
Lehnert and Landrock
44 Sharia Sherif, downtown.
Tel: (202) 3935324.
L'Orientaliste
Nile Hilton Annexe
Tel: (202) 5762440.
Diwan
159 26th July St, Zamalek

Reproduction of an original painting on papyrus

Tel: (202) 7362588; email: info@diwanegypt.com

Brass and copper
The shops in the Coppersmiths' Bazaar are the places for brass and copperware. You will find both these items at the western end of Khan el Khalili, along Sharia Muizz, between Sharia Muski and the Madrasa of Sultan Qalaun.

Camels
The camel bazaar, Souk el Gamel, is at Birqash beyond the Imbaba district of northwest Cairo, and is best reached by taxi. The market is held every Friday from 6am; the activity is pretty much over by 9am. Docile females are the preferred mounts, for which you should expect to pay LE2,500.

Clothing and fabrics
Abbas Higazi
Top-quality cloth and ready-to-wear or tailor-made traditional garments.
Khan el Khalili.
Tel: (202) 5924730.

Ammar
Good-quality traditional
galabiyya.
26 Sharia Qasr el Nil.

Atlas
Ready-to-wear, made-to-
measure clothes, and
fabrics also available.
*Sikket el Badestan, at the
heart of Khan el Khalili.
Tel: (202) 5906139.*

Nomad
Bedouin designs adapted
to Western styles.
*Marriott Hotel, Zamalek.
Tel: (202) 7283000.
14 Sariya el Gezira,
Zamalek.
Tel: (202) 7362132.*

Omar Effendi
Department store.
*Downtown branches on
Sharia Talaat Harb just
off Midan el Tahrir, and
on Sharia Adli near
Sharia Talaat Harb.*

On Safari
Stylish casual clothing.
*10 Sharia Lutfalla,
Zamalek.
Tel: (202) 7351909.*

Gifts
Khan Misr Toulon
*Opposite Ibn Tulun
Mosque, and just up the
street from Gayer-
Anderson House.
17 Ahmed Ibn Tulun St,*
*near Citadel.
Tel: (202) 3652227.*

Jewellery
Nomad
Bedouin jewellery.
*Marriott Hotel, Zamalek.
Tel: (202) 7283000.
14 Saraya el Gezira.
Tel: (202) 7362132.*

Sirgany
Gold.
*Sharia el Sagha, Khan el
Khalili. Tel: (202)
5901255.*

Leather, shoes and accessories
There is a plethora of
bags, belts, suitcases and
shoe shops on Sharias
26 July, Talaat Harb and
Kasr el Nil, while leather
goods and accessories are
widely sold in Khan el
Khalili market.

Musical instruments
Shops sell traditional
instruments on Sharia el
Qa'la between Midan
Ataba and the Islamic
Art Museum.

Papyrus
**Dr Ragab's Papyrus
Institute**
*On a houseboat moored
south of the Giza*
*Sheraton.
Tel: (202) 3488676.*

Scents and spices
Khan el Khalili's spice
and perfume bazaars are
in the southeast quadrant
formed by the junction
of Sharia el Muizz and
Sharia el Muski, though
spilling beyond.

Silver
Saad of Egypt
Silver.
*Ramses Hilton.
Tel: (202) 5754999.
Khan el Khalili.
Tel: (202) 5893992.*

Weavings, carpets, tents and tapestries
The tent-makers' bazaar
is on Sharia Muizz,
immediately south of
Bab Zuwayla.

Senouhi
All kinds of carpets –
an exclusive outlet for
Harraniyya tapestries.
*5th floor, 54 Sharia Abdel
Khalek Sarwat,
downtown. Tel: (202)
3910955.*

Woodwork and inlay
**Mother-of-Pearl
Products**
6 Khan el Khalili.

Entertainment

With the almost complete disappearance of its formerly cosmopolitan population since the 1950s, the range, quantity and distribution of entertainment in Egypt have become much reduced. Alexandria, once full of Greeks, Italians, Jews, English, French and others, now has virtually no nightlife or cultural activity that the passing visitor would notice. With the exception of Cairo, the same is true throughout the country, unless a luxury hotel lays on a tourist show. In Cairo there is entertainment until the early hours, and it is a special pleasure at the end of a long night out to see the sun come up while the calls for dawn prayers echo across the city.

Many well-to-do Egyptians attend ballet, opera and concerts at Cairo's Opera House. Foreign cultural centres such as the British Council offer films, music and theatre. It is even possible to go tenpin bowling and ice-skating.

However, visitors on a short stay may not have the time or inclination to seek these events out. Folk entertainments are still staged, in specialist theatres and large hotels, but more rewarding can be those genuine manifestations of popular culture, the *moulids* and other festivals (*see pp22–3*).

Visitors, therefore, should understand that even in Cairo the hotels are the best bet for entertainment, and that outside Cairo there is virtually nowhere else to go. The monthly magazines *Egypt Today* and *Community Times*, and the weekly English-language edition of *Al-Ahram* will give you a fairly good idea of what is going on.

What's on offer

Almost all bars are within hotels or form part of a restaurant or nightclub. Many will have some form of entertainment. While the consumption of alcohol is legal, it is illegal to serve Egyptians (be they Copts or Muslims) during Ramadan or other festivals, which means bars not in international hotels are likely to be closed then. Cairo, however, does have a number of bars scattered around the city.

Casinos

Admission to casinos, found in many major hotels, is restricted to non-Egyptians. The currency to play is US dollars, with free drinks to punters. Doors close at dawn.

Cinemas

English-language films are frequently shown, subtitled in Arabic. Sometimes the Egyptian audience, being able to read the subtitles, does not have to listen to the dialogue, but chatters away instead, making it difficult for others to hear, but audiences are becoming better-behaved. Prices are very reasonable.

Discos

Almost all discos are at the major hotels, and many of these are restricted to guests or members. Women will usually have no trouble entering alone, but men will often find that they cannot enter without a woman. You should phone first to check. As with bars, there are several discos.

Egyptian dance and music

El Jeel is the rhythmic pop music of Egypt, a blend of Nubian, Bedouin and Libyan beats. Live performances are sometimes included in nightclub programmes at Cairo's major hotels, or downtown, or along the Pyramids Road. Classical Arab music is presented at Cairo's Sayed Darwish Concert Hall in Gîza, while folkloric music and dance are presented at the Balloon Theatre in the Cairo district of Agouza.

Nightclubs

The best nightclubs are found in Cairo's main international hotels. They usually offer a programme of both oriental and Western acts, for example, a first-class Egyptian belly dancer between thick slices of second-rate pseudo-Las Vegas showgirl acts. A four-course dinner is served from about 8pm onwards, the belly dancer usually coming on late, at about 11pm. Reservations are required.

Opera, ballet and theatre

The Cairo Opera House is home to the Cairo Ballet Company, the Cairo Opera Company and the Cairo Symphony Orchestra, and is the venue for visiting operas, plays and musicals. Special events are often staged at the Pyramids, for example, operas and pop concerts.

Entertainment at a Cairo nightclub

Where to go

Entertainment in Cairo is not hard to find, with bars, discos, restaurants and nightclubs aplenty to suit all tastes. Opera, ballet, concerts and theatre are all on offer. For detailed information, a publication worth buying is *Cairo's Top 1000*, a guide to drinking, dining and dancing.

Bars

Barrel Lounge
A pleasant atmosphere and an interesting variety of clientele.
First floor, Windsor Hotel, Sharia Alfi Bey.

Absolute
Popular bar with music.
9 Amman Square, Mohandessin.
Tel: (202) 7497326.

Pub 28
Modelled on the traditional British pub.
28 Shagar el Durr, Zamalek.

Jazz Up
Pub with attitude.
Nile Hilton Hotel, Midan el Tahrir.
Tel: (202) 5780444.

Windows on the World
Fantastic views over Cairo.

Ramses Hilton Hotel, Corniche el Nil, Boulaq.
Tel: (202) 5777444.

Casinos

The Casino
Busy until the early hours.
Nile Hilton Hotel, Corniche el Nil, downtown.
Tel: (202) 5780444.

Casino Semiramis
Semiramis Intercontinental Hotel, Corniche el Nil, Garden City.
Tel: (202) 7957171.

Omar Khayyam Casino
Cairo Marriott Hotel, Zamalek.
Tel: (202) 7283000.

Cinemas

Cairo has a plethora of cinemas in a number of locations – hotels, shopping malls, downtown and the suburbs, all showing the latest American and British films, as well as Egyptian productions. The foreign cultural centres, for example the British Council, at *192 Sharia el Nil, Agouza, Tel: (202) 3453281,* sometimes show films.

Discos

Latex
A disco situated in the 5-star Nile Hilton.
Nile Hilton Hotel, Midan el Tahrir.
Tel: (202) 5780444.

Hard Rock Café
Next to Grand Hyatt Hotel, Corniche El Nil, Garden City.
Tel: (202) 5321285.

Egyptian music and dance

Balloon Theatre
Venue for the National Troupe and the Reda Troupe, both folk dance troupes.
Sharia 26 July at Sharia el Nil, Agouza.
Tel: (202) 3471718.

Sayed Darwish Concert Hall
Venue for the Arabic Music Troupe.
Gamal el Din el Afghani, near the City of Art.
Tel: (202) 5612473.

Nightclubs

Arizona
If you are looking for the bottom of the barrel, this is it: sagging bellies and other grotesqueries.
El Haram Street.

Haroun el Rashid
Different shows nightly.
*Semiramis
Intercontinental Hotel,
Corniche el Nil, Garden
City. Tel: (202) 7957171.*
El Leil
Rather downmarket bar,
and belly-dancing show.
El Haram Street, Giza.

Opera, ballet and theatre
Cairo Opera House
A Japanese-designed
complex. The ballet

season runs from
January onwards,
opera from March
onwards, and the
symphony orchestra
season from September
through to June.
*On Gezira Island in
Zamalek.*
Tel: (202) 7370601.
info@cairooperahouse.org
Gomhouria Theatre
Plays in various
languages including
English, French and
Arabic.

*12 Sharia Gumhuria,
downtown.*
Tel: (202) 3919956.
Wallace Theatre
English-language plays
and musicals are
performed here, as
well as concerts,
though only during
the academic year
from October through
to May.
*American University in
Cairo, Sharia Kasr el Aini,
off Midan el Tahrir.*
Tel: (202) 7976105.

The Cairo Ballet Company and Symphony Orchestra perform in the Cairo Opera House

Popular entertainment

A dancing baboon, a woman breathing fire, a man staging a backstreet performance involving a snake and a guinea pig, these are among the forms of entertainment you might come across on the streets of Cairo or Alexandria. Weddings are also a public spectacle, the parade of ululating women, tambourine-playing men, usually a belly dancer, too, preceding the bashful bride and groom. The form is similar whether along the streets of the poorer quarters, or through the lobby of a luxury hotel.

You might sit at a café like Fishawi's in Khan el Khalili and listen to a gypsy woman singing a wailing song, or go to a low dive like the Arizona at the Midan Orabi end of Sharia Alfi to watch belly dancers who've seen better days. A zany finger-cymbal player is followed by a nonchalant Lebanese riding a unicycle across a wire 2m (6$\frac{1}{2}$ft) above the stage. What is common to all these entertainments, the puppet shows, the story tellings, and the dervish hoppings that accompany every *moulid*, is the abandoned enjoyment with which they are each equally received.

It is perhaps this playfulness, together with a flair for the melodramatic and a touch of African oomph, that makes Egyptians the leading film makers, actors, dancers and singers in the entire Arab world.

The long-robed Kuwaitis, Saudis and Sudanese are not in the big city to attend the El Azhar; they have come for fun. Cairo has long been the Hollywood, the La Scala, the Motown and the Las Vegas of the Middle East. Even in the warble of the muezzins there is a virtuosity unheard elsewhere. It can be traced back to the drones and chants of the Coptic Church, some of whose own hymns almost certainly preserve something from forms of ancient pharaonic worship.

A display of Sufi dancing

Performances of belly dancing can be seen in the major hotels

Children

Egyptians are extremely indulgent towards children, and you will find that they are welcomed everywhere, including hotels and restaurants, mosques and archaeological sites. However, this lack of fussiness can expose a child to accidents. Be alert to untended excavations and traffic, for example, and be sure that your children observe careful hygiene and are well protected with clothing, hats and sunglasses against the sun. The better hotels can usually provide childminders, and medical services are excellent.

Children will probably find the dress, the scent and the bustle of the bazaar more interesting than a museum or tomb. Carriage and camel rides, and sailing in a *felucca* are particular favourites. Sound and light shows will be mysterious and fun. Floating and outdoor restaurants will seem novel, and certain themed eating places out by the pyramids have been designed with children very much in mind. Additionally, there are a number of attractions which are aimed especially at children.

Aquarium Grotto Gardens

Numerous marine tanks, spread along a labyrinth of passageways in the Grotto, referred to as the Fish Garden, contain nearly 200 varieties of fascinating tropical fish and sea creatures. The pretty gardens contain two lakes.
Gabalaya Park, Zamalek.
Open: daily 8.30am–3.30pm.
Admission charge.

El Azhar Park

This lush, green oasis provides magnificent views of the citadel and surrounding mosques. One of its star attractions is the newly excavated Ayyubid Wall, built by Salah El Din to protect the city. The park's restaurants and cafés are ideal places to relax.
Entrance off the Salah Salem Rd near the Citadel. Tel: (202) 5103868.
www.alazharpark.com. Open
8.30am–midnight. Admission charge.

Cairo Puppet Theatre

Puppet shows regularly held here, including old favourites like *Ali Baba* and *Sinbad*, are in Arabic. It hardly matters, though, as it is very easy to follow the action.

The season is from October through to May, with performances at 6pm on Thursdays and Fridays only.
Midan Ataba at the southeast end of Ezbekieh Gardens, downtown.
Tel: (202) 5910954.

Cairo Zoo

An extensive and well-stocked zoo – the finest in the world when it was founded a century ago – but sadly not very well kept now. There are pony rides.
Gîza. Open: daily 6am–5pm. Admission charge.

Dr Ragab's Pharaonic Village

A two-hour tour takes you round a replica temple and nobleman's villa, and floats you along the Canal of Mythology where you encounter the ancient gods. There is also a mock-up of King Tutankhamun's tomb, several museums, a playground and a restaurant.
Jacob Island. Tel: (202) 5718675. Reached by half-hourly boats from the Corniche el Nil, 2km (1¼ miles) south of Gîza Bridge. Open: daily 9am–9pm. Admission charge, but free for children under six.

Felfela Village

This rambling outdoor entertainment complex is popular with children, and has a restaurant, playground, camel rides, a puppet show and zoo, plus a programme including acrobats, music, belly dancers and dancing horses, only on Fridays.
Maryotteya Canal, Gîza. Tel: (202) 3841111. Open: 10am–7pm. Admission charge.

National Circus

A good one-ring affair with the usual animals, acrobats and clowns.
Next to the Balloon Theatre at Agouza, by the 26 July Bridge.

Tel: (202) 3470612. Daily performances from 8.30pm. Admission charge.

Sinbad Amusement Park

Bigger than the Cookie Amusement Park near the pyramids, this has bumper cars, a roller-coaster and other rides.
Near Cairo Airport. Open: summer, daily 5pm–2am, winter, daily 2–11pm, except Fri when it opens at 10am. Admission charge.

El Urman Gardens

These former gardens of the khedives of Egypt provide plenty of space for kids to enjoy a picnic after a visit to the zoo, if a little run-down.
Gîza, opposite Cairo Zoo. Open: daily 8am–8pm, closes Thur at noon, and all day Fri. Admission charge.

Confident on camel-back

Sport and leisure

Apart from the Red Sea resorts, with their almost exclusive concentration on diving activities, the main centre for sport is Cairo, which provides well for visitors wanting to keep fit or have fun. However, in most tourist resorts, for example Luxor, Sharm and Hurghada, tennis and golf are both available.

The all-round choice

The best all-round place is the Gezira Sporting Club, the oldest and most distinguished club in Cairo. Founded in 1888, it was built primarily for the British and a select number of Egyptians, and offered, then as now, such sports as polo and croquet. With the 1952 revolution, however, most foreign members were thrown out, and Egyptians were more freely admitted, although today it still has more foreign members than any other club in Cairo.

The Club has many sports to offer, but visitors are restricted to enjoying just two: golf and horse racing. There is a nine-hole golf course with a small pro shop where you can hire equipment. Horse racing takes place every alternate Saturday and Sunday (every other Saturday it is at the Heliopolis Hippodrome).

Gezira Sporting Club, Sharia Gezira, Zamalek. Tel: (202) 7352272.
Open: 7am–11pm.
Admission charge.

Cycling

Cairo and its environs offer a diverse range of enjoyable and unique cycling venues. Organised road rides take place every Friday morning at 7am, leaving from the front gate of Cairo American College, 1 Midan Digla, Maadi. Off-road rides also occur most Saturday mornings at 7am, departing from the front gate of CAC. Riders of all ages, levels of interest and ability are encouraged to join in.

For information and details contact
www.cairocyclists.com

Diving

The **Maadi Dive Centre** meets on a regular basis and runs courses for visitors and residents alike.

For information contact Magdi on 010 100 4628, or email mdivers@intouch. com, www.maadi-divers.com

Golf

There are about a dozen golf courses in Cairo, and at major resorts around

Egypt. One of the oldest, the Mena House course, is a well-watered oasis beneath the brown of the Pyramids. However, one of the best courses in Cairo is **Mirage**, an 18-hole course on the outskirts of the city and, like its near neighbour, purpose-built in the desert. Both Mirage and **Katamaya** have opulent clubhouses with attendant health-club facilities, swimming and tennis. Both clubs are around 25km (16 miles) from Cairo city centre.

Out of Cairo, there are some stunning courses, most notably at Soma Bay on the Red Sea, and, further north, the course at El Gouna.

Mirage City Golf Club, Ring Road, new Cairo. Tel: (202) 4091464.

Health clubs

All the luxury-class hotels have health clubs. Hotel residents have automatic temporary membership; many admit non-residents on a daily or weekly basis.

Nile Hilton Health Club

Facilities include a gymnasium, sauna, swimming pool and tennis courts.

Nile Hilton Hotel, Midan el Tahrir. Tel: (202) 5780444. Open: daily 10am–10pm. Charges vary according to facility used.

Splash

Swimming pool, Jacuzzi, floodlit tennis courts, health-food bar, etc.

Marriott Hotel, Zamalek. Tel: (202) 7283000. Open: daily 6am–11pm. Charges vary according to facility used.

Running

The **Cairo Hash House Harriers** meet every Friday afternoon approximately two hours before sunset all year round. Run, jog, walk in locations near Cairo such as Wadi Digla, the Petrified Forest or near the Pyramids.

For information and contact details, see www.cairohash.com

Spectator sports

Maadi Runners

The Maadi Runners run for fun and the enjoyment of meeting other people and are a multinational crowd living in Egypt. If you love to run, whether for fun or with a marathon in mind, join in every Friday morning in front of the CAC in Maadi. (*See Cairo Cycling Club for details.*) Runs can be to the Sphinx, from Saqqâra to Dashur, or may take place out of Cairo.

For details contact Mohsen Alashmoni at mohsen.a@internetegypt.com

Football and horse racing

Information on spectator sports is found in the newspaper *The Egyptian Gazette (The Egyptian Mail)*.

Egypt's favourite sport is football. The two main teams are Zamalek and Ahly. From September through to May, games are played every weekend (Friday–Sunday) at the Cairo Stadium in Heliopolis. There is horse racing from October to May at the Gezira Sporting Club and the Heliopolis Hippodrome.

Red Sea reefs

The Red Sea offers perfect conditions for the growth of coral. As well as having a high water temperature, which in itself promotes growth, the depth of the Red Sea prevents surface waves from affecting reef development. No major rivers spill into the sea, so its waters are exceptionally clear, allowing sunlight to penetrate deeply. As a result, Red Sea reefs extend deeper than in most other coral areas.

Most visiting divers stay within the fringe reef. A shallow sandy lagoon extends from the shoreline to the reef crest, a zone often too shallow for fish to cross. It is commonly the home of organ pipe corals. Beyond this is the reef slope, which is very steep and occasionally overhanging, with deep

Exploring the coral reefs

The Red Sea reefs are home to a fascinating array of marine life

caves and canyons. Here, there are massive banks of mountain and staghorn corals. Further out, the fore reef now descends more gradually, almost horizontally, covered by unusual coral formations which can rise close to the surface.

Corals

Coral reefs constitute the most complex community of animals and plants in the sea. Many species of fish, from jewel-like damselfish to brightly spotted snappers, make their home here, taking advantage of the abundance and variety of food organisms, as well as the shelter the reef affords from predators, although some, such as the ferocious moray eel, do lurk in its crevices.

Adjacent seagrasses are important as a nursery ground for many reef fish, while fish living in the sand flats beyond, such as rays or lizardfish, are either protectively coloured to look like sand, or they actually bury themselves in it.

Rules

• To preserve the fragile reefs, the rule, enforced by law, is never to take anything out of them, dead or alive.
• For your own safety, you should wear protective covering on your feet, you should not touch the coral, and you should not swim alone.
• Never buy products made from reef creatures.

Cruising

Taking a cruise along the Nile is a time-honoured tradition. It can be the journey of a lifetime and is one of the best ways of seeing the ancient sites in Upper Egypt. For the adventurous, sailing along the Nile in a felucca *is the thing (see pp132–3). If you prefer not to trust to sail and sleeping bag, there is the comfort of the traditional cruise. A Nile cruise may form part of an overall package, or you may be an independent traveller who wants to include a cruise in your plans. It is possible to arrange both from abroad and, indeed, it would be wisest if you did so. Once in Egypt, you will be leaving it to the last moment and you will have to take whatever, if anything, is available.*

Travel agencies such as Thomas Cook or the Egyptian agency Misr Travel can make the arrangements either in Egypt or abroad (*see p185*). Cruise operators include Thomas Cook, Presidential Nile Cruises, Abercrombie & Kent, Explore

Your towels will often be rearranged in Egyptian hotels and cruisers

Worldwide, Kuoni and Swan Hellenic. Several groups also operate cruises which can be booked through their hotels or reservation centres.

Prices

Prices are highest from October to May, falling by about ten per cent in summer, and include meals, sightseeing ashore, taxes and service charges. For a five-day cruise on one of the international hotel chain boats, expect to pay about $1,600 per double cabin during high season, and about $1,300 during low season. Local operators offer cruises at substantially lower rates.

Floating hotels

The international hotel boats, known as 'floating hotels', are the behemoths of the Nile. With 26 to 80 cabins, bars, boutiques, swimming pools, hairdressers and discos, they can leave you uncertain about whether you ever left dry land. On the larger boats, you may feel, however, that their luxury, and the number of people on board, gets in the way of the experience.

Often the smaller the boat, the better the ambience. There are several vessels of 20 to 30 cabins that are used both by local and overseas operators, and time and again it is these less prepossessing craft which win the most enthusiastic reactions from travellers.

The itinerary

A cruise on the Nile, seeing life along its banks, has a profound cumulative effect on you. There are innumerable cruise boats on the Nile, the majority plying between Luxor and Aswân, and calling at Esna, Edfu and Kom Ombo. Some loop northwards from Luxor to visit Dendera and Abydos. Most cruises are four to eight days long, though half that time is spent moored at Luxor or Aswân while you trot round the local sites. Sadly, the full cruise between Cairo and Aswân is currently suspended, with no plans to reinstate it. All cruises include the services of an Egyptian guide who will be trained in archaeological history, but their quality can be variable. Some foreign-organised cruises will also include the services of a qualified Egyptologist who will give lectures and can answer questions. Enquire closely to ensure that your cruise provides you with the level of scholarly backup that you want.

Cruise ship on the Nile

Food and drink

From simple village fare to classic Turkish cuisine, with Greek, Lebanese and French influences, Egyptian food is as varied as the country's history, geography and social structure. Most hotels in Egypt, however, cater to the tastes of foreign visitors by serving an international cuisine, so that if you want to immerse yourself in the full variety of Egyptian cooking you need to venture forth to the multitude of restaurants serving from the humblest to the most exquisite meals. A dining guide to Cairo's top 500 restaurants can be purchased in hotel book shops and all good stationers.

Variety of choice

Typically, dishes will be savoury, neither too oily nor too spicy, and because only fresh ingredients will be used, the menu will vary with the season. Nubian cooking, in the south of Egypt, tends to be spicier; Alexandrian cuisine is Mediterranean. In Cairo, the choice is almost limitless. There are no specific vegetarian restaurants in Egypt. However, most places will have something for those who cannot eat meat, poultry or fish.

Eating places can be divided into four broad categories. There are Western-style restaurants which generally aim at a diluted or internationalised French cuisine. They will have a correspondingly wide-ranging menu. Then there are speciality restaurants – Greek, Chinese, Japanese, Italian, Indian, or those pretending to be a pharaonic barge – which tend to offer one fare, with some variations and alternatives. Also, there are Middle Eastern restaurants which run the gamut from simple Egyptian fare through to Levantine, which can be a mixture of Egyptian, Turkish, French and other cuisines. In addition, there are cafés where you can get a light meal. Egypt has its fair share of fast-food restaurants, and these proliferate from Alexandria to Aswân. Wherever and whatever you decide to eat, be scrupulous about hygiene, and never eat anything that has been lying around, or is improperly cooked or washed.

National dishes

Egypt's national dishes include *fool*, a paste made from the fava bean to which oil, lemon, salt and pepper are usually added. *Tamaiya* (*felafel*) is made from the same beans, but in this case they are pressed into a patty and fried in oil. *Tahina* is a sesame paste, while *babaganouh* is a paste made from aubergines. *Koushari* is a delicious mixture of rice, macaroni, lentils and chickpeas, topped with a spicy sauce, and *molokhia*, a spinach-like plant, is cooked as a soup or sauce. Meat usually comes as kebabs and *kofta*, a spicy ground meat patty.

One or several of these dishes will be the entire offering of the simplest Egyptian eating places. Probably there will be no menu, but you can always go into the kitchen, have a look, a taste, and then point to what you want.

As these are national dishes, you will probably find them, even if only as *hors d'oeuvres*, on the menu of almost any restaurant in the country.

Drinks

Turkish-style coffee, thick and black, is ordered according to the amount of sugar: sweet (*ziyada*), medium (*mazboota*), or bitter (*saada*). Western-style brewed coffee is usually called 'American coffee', while instant coffee is almost always known as 'Nescafé' whether it is or not. Tea is generally understood as mint tea or Indian tea, but usually without milk.

Western-style soft drinks, including Coca-Cola and 7-Up, are available everywhere. Egypt scores well on tropical fruit and cane juices. Tap water in the towns is heavily chlorinated, and so it is more for reasons of taste than safety that you might prefer to buy bottled mineral water.

Stella beer in both the green can and the green bottle is very good. Stella Export, Sakkara and Meister beer are all sweeter, stronger and more expensive. Egyptian wines have improved dramatically and there are several brands. A very drinkable dry white is Shahrazade, which also comes in a very palatable red and rosé. Grand Marquis is more expensive, the white being dry and the red full bodied, and the Obelisk range competes quite favourably. There are more wines on the market, including the upscale Château des Rêves and, for those who like a bit of fizz, the sparkling wine, Aïda, is really very drinkable.

It's worth noting that imported beers, wines and spirits are very expensive so it's well worth trying the local varieties. Wine and beer can be bought from several outlets, including any Thomas delicatessen/café and Drinkies, a shop specially licensed to sell alcohol.

Egypt makes its own spirits, which are perfectly acceptable, although steer clear of gin and whisky with names which are a juxtaposition of the original, e.g. Gorder's Gin. These can be dangerous and should not be touched. However, properly licensed whisky, gin and vodka sold in specifically licensed shops are all palatable, and arak (the Arab equivalent of Greek ouzo) is excellent whether neat, on the rocks or diluted with water.

Food and drink

Where to eat

In Upper Egypt and at the Red Sea resorts it is the hotels which offer the best eating places, although there are now more and more independent restaurants springing up in these areas. Unfortunately, some are dull and, in several cases, definitely unacceptable. However, in Cairo and, to a lesser extent, Alexandria, there is a wide choice of cuisine and atmosphere.

Cairo is more expensive than Alexandria, and generally hotel restaurants are more expensive than others. Drinks in hotels are generally fairly expensive, and a bottle of wine can be more than double the retail cost.

Generally speaking, a bottle of local wine will retail at about LE40 in one of the special shops licensed to sell alcohol. A bottle of local wine with a meal might cost in the region of LE100, becoming slightly cheaper according to the standard of the restaurant.

The following ratings will give a rough indication of the cost of a two-course meal for one person, without alcohol:

★	cheap	LE20–40
★★	mid-range	LE40–85
★★★	expensive	LE85–150+

ALEXANDRIA
Western-style food
El Farouk ★★★
Very stylish, fine dining with a French flavour, the restaurant is in the El Salamlek Palace Hotel, situated in the beautiful grounds of the Montazah Palace.
Montazah Palace Gardens, Montazah.
Tel: (203) 5477999.

Delta Hotel Restaurant ★★
Excellent French cuisine.
14 Sharia Champollion, Mazarita.
Tel: (203) 4869053.

Lord's Inn ★★★
Posh, romantic, and good food.
Sharia Mohammed Ahmed el Afifi, San Stefano.
Tel: (203) 5462016.

Tikka Grill and Fish Market ★★
The best setting in Alexandria, with marvellous views over the Eastern Harbour. The varied menu includes seafood, grills, soups and salads.
Tariq el Gheish el Kashafa el Baharia Club.
Tel: (203) 4805114.

Speciality restaurants
Chez Gaby au Ritrovo ★★
Popular restaurant serving good pizzas and pasta. Will deliver.
Closed Mon.

ALCOHOL IN EGYPT

The consumption of alcohol is legal in Egypt, though an Egyptian cannot buy a drink during Ramadan, and some governorates are dry all year round. Neither EgyptAir nor the railways serve alcoholic drinks. That being said, alcoholic drinks are readily available at hotels and most restaurants – ask and you will receive. Beer, wine and spirits are only sold in specially licensed shops. Egypt now sells gin, whisky and vodka that is perfectly acceptable for around LE90, but do not buy cheap, locally produced spirits.

22 Sharia el Hurriya.
Tel: (203) 4846329.

China House ★★

One of Alexandria's
Chinese-only
restaurants.
Carrebour. Tel: (203)
4877173.

El Farida Restaurant ★★

Also located in the
El-Salamlek Palace
Hotel, El Farida
specialises in Italian
food, although
international cuisine
is also available.
Montazah Palace
Gardens, Montazah.
Tel: (203) 5477999.

Sea Gull ★★

Built like a castle,
dedicated to seafood.
Sharia Agami, Mex.
Tel: (203) 4405575.

Middle Eastern

El Ekhlaas ★★

Very good oriental
cuisine.
49 Sharia Safiya
Zaghloul. Tel: (203)
4864434.

**Fuul Mohammed
Ahmed** ★

The best place for cheap,
simple Egyptian
specialities.
317 Sharia Shaker.
Tel: (203) 4873576.

Café-restaurants
Athineos ★

Café, patisserie and light
meals served at this one-
time Greek place, ornate
though overly refurbished.
21 Midan Sa'ad Zaghlul.
Tel: (203) 4868131.

Pastroudis ★★

Founded in 1923, this,
along with the Cecil
Hotel, is the Alexandrian
institution most
mentioned in Lawrence
Durrell's Alexandria
Quartet. Restaurant,
patisserie and
indoor/outdoor café.
39 Sharia el Hurriya.
Tel: (203) 3929609.

Trianon ★★

Indoor café, patisserie
and restaurant; Art
Nouveau décor. This was
a favourite haunt of the

Pastroudis – one of
Alexandria's institutions

poet Cavafy, whose office
was in the building above.
Midan Sa'ad Zaghlul.
Tel: (203) 4868539.

CAIRO
Western-style food
La Bodega ★★

Located in a beautiful,
belle époque building, this
busy restaurant is
evocative of the
exuberant Twenties.
Tasty continental and
international food,
reasonably priced, is
served here. Reservations
recommended.
157 26th July St, 1st floor,
Zamalek. Tel: (202)
7350543.

La Chesa ★★

Operated by Swissair
Restaurants, this is a
haven of Swiss
cleanliness, excellent
food, and a fine cake and
pastry section.
21 Sharia Adli,
downtown. Tel: (202)
3939360.

Estoril ★

French food in plain
surroundings but served
by elaborately costumed
Nubians.
12 Sharia Talaat Harb,
downtown.
Tel: (202) 5743102.

Justine ★★★

Reputed to be one of the best and one of the most expensive restaurants in Cairo, the cuisine is international, and the atmosphere formal.
4 Sharia Hassan Sabri, Zamalek.
Tel: (202) 7362961.

Khan al-Khalili ★★

In the heart of the bazaar, this restaurant serves European and Egyptian food. Good for snacks, and has the cleanest toilets in the area. No alcohol served.
5 Sikkat el Badistan, Khan el Khalili.
Tel: (202) 5903788.

Speciality restaurants

Asiatique ★★

A popular restaurant serving excellent Chinese, Thai and Japanese cuisine in elegant surroundings on board *Le Pacha* boat, moored in Zamalek. Reasonably priced, and it is best to book.
Le Pacha Boat, Saraya el Gezira, Zamalek.
Tel: (202) 7356730.

Fish Market Americana Boat ★★

Choose your own fish on this popular boat moored on the Nile.
26 Nile Street, Agonza.
Tel: (202) 5709693.

Kandahar ★★

Indian food eaten to the accompaniment of Indian music.
3 Gammat El Dowal St, Mohandessin.
Tel: (202) 3030615.

The Nile Pharaoh ★★★

A cruising restaurant that looks like a pharaonic sailing barge. Operated by the Oberoi Hotels group, owners of the Mena House. There are both lunch and dinner cruises.
For reservations and boarding directions, tel: (202) 5701000.

La Piazza ★★

A light and airy, trattoria-style restaurant with friendly waiters, Mediterranean/Italian food and good service. Reasonably priced and open for lunch and dinner. Located in the Four Corners building next door to Justine, beside the Crédit Agricole Bank.
4 Hassan Sabry St, Zamalek.
Tel: (202) 7362961

Middle Eastern restaurants

Abou El Sid ★★

The best Middle Eastern and Mediterranean cuisine in town. The dark interior is a witty mix of French and Oriental décor, and *nargiles* are available but it's not too smoky. A modern restaurant for those who love a

Eating in style in an expensive restaurant

traditional feel.
Essential to book.
*Just round the corner
from 157 26th July St,
Zamalek. (Door sign
reads 'Charmerie'), up
a few steps to a huge
doorway.
Tel: (202) 7359640.*

Arabesque ★★

This is an elegant
restaurant with a small
friendly bar; adjoining
it is a small gallery of
works by Egyptian
artists. The cuisine is
Egyptian, Lebanese and
Continental. Prices are
moderate, but drinking
imported wine will make
it expensive.
*6 Sharia Qasr el Nil,
downtown.
Tel: (202) 5747898.*

Casino des Pigeons ★★

Pigeon and chicken,
grilled or stuffed, with
good *hors d'oeuvres* and
salads. The dining is
either outdoors among
palms and papyrus or
inside. No alcohol served.
*155 Bahr el Azam, near
the Giza Bridge, Giza.
Tel: (202) 5721299.*

Felfela ★

Though popular with
tourists and foreign
residents, it is also a

Take time out to have a cup of tea, especially with mint

favourite with Egyptians,
and the food is certainly
good. Tree trunks serve
as tables. The speciality
is *fool* in all its varied
preparations, but the
menu extends to
meat dishes, ice
creams, etc.
*15 Sharia Hoda Sharawi,
just off Sharia Talaat
Harb. Tel: (202) 3922751.*

**Odeon Palace Hotel
Restaurant ★**

A 24-hour restaurant
and bar appealing to
journalists, actors,
artists and tourists.
The food is typical
Egyptian fare.
*6 Sharia Abd el Hamid
Shahad, off Sharia Talaat
Harb, downtown.
Tel: (202) 5767971.*

Cafés

Egypt, and Cairo
especially, is very much a
café society. Along with a
proliferation of
traditional coffee shops,
there are a number of
chains which include
Beanos, Costa Coffee,
Cinnabon and Coffee
Roastery, to name but a
few. However, one classic
café deserves a special
mention. Fishawi's,
Cairo's oldest teahouse, is
one café you should not
miss for its atmosphere
of old Cairo. It is in a
small alley running
parallel to the west side
of the square in front
of the Sayyidna el
Hussein Mosque in
Khan el Khalili.

Hotels and accommodation

The number of hotels in Egypt has increased tremendously over the past ten years, although most are still in established centres and at the upper end of the market. The most rapid development has been at the Red Sea resorts and in Sinai. Middle-category accommodation has also increased, especially in Cairo. However, it is still a good idea to make advance reservations – in Upper Egypt, the Red Sea and Sinai during the winter; in Alexandria during the summer; or, if you have your heart set on a particular hotel, anywhere, at any time.

Reservations can be made through Thomas Cook or another good travel agent. The international chain hotels can be booked by contacting one of their hotels or reservation centres in your own country. You may be asked to deposit a credit card.

Bear in mind that some areas of the country, such as the Delta, and along the Nile, apart from Minya, Luxor and Aswân, will only rarely have any decent hotels. In these areas, plan your tour in terms of centres from which you can make day excursions. A Nile cruise (see pp162–3) is another way of getting round the problem. It is usually less expensive to buy an all-inclusive package than to make your own arrangements.

Star rating

Hotels in Egypt are officially rated from 5-star (luxury) to 1-star. The rating system is not always evenly graduated, however, and you may find that a 3-star hotel is just as good as a 4-star one, or that two 4-star hotels, even in the same place, vary in quality and charge markedly different rates. As a rule of thumb, any hotel from three stars upwards will be acceptable; below that you should inspect the place and your room before committing yourself.

There are also hotels that have no star ratings, and also youth hostels.

Old Winter Palace, Luxor

Modern and spacious: top-quality hotels carry 5-star ratings

By and large these should be given a wide berth, though you will occasionally learn through word of mouth of some place that is acceptable.

The bill

In addition to the basic charge for a room, service charges and tax together amount to between 15 and 20 per cent. Breakfast is often an obligatory extra. Single rooms or single occupancy of a double room cost 10 to 20 per cent less than the doubles rate. Rates in Cairo are often higher than elsewhere, and remain roughly the same year-round. In Alexandria they are about ten per cent lower in winter; in Upper Egypt, the Red Sea and Sinai they are about ten per cent lower in summer. Other factors affecting rates include the view and, in the lower categories, bath facilities in the room.

Hotels quote room rates both in US dollars and Egyptian pounds. Here they are given in dollars.

Double room rates in Cairo

5-star: $160–$210+
4-star: $110–$160
3-star: $75–$110
2-star: $35–$75
1-star: up to $35

Double room rates elsewhere

5-star: $110–$160+
4-star: $60–$110
3-star: $40–$60
2-star: $25–$40
1-star: up to $25

At Coptic monasteries there is no charge, though a donation would not go amiss. Accommodation is clean and basic. For further details on staying at Coptic monasteries, see *p178*.

CRUISE BOOKING

A number of boats of all categories are privately owned by hotels and other companies in Egypt, and keep changing all the time. For information regarding Nile or Lake Nasser cruises contact Thomas Cook in Egypt, your nearest travel agent, or use the internet.

Egypt's legendary hotels

In the pre-air-conditioned age of grand tourism, from the late 19th century to the mid-20th century, Egypt boasted a number of gloriously cavernous hotels where sunlight filtered through louvred doors and mosquito nets wavered in the evening breezes. Garden sounds and fragrances crept into the rooms, along with the occasional beetle and drift of sand. There was an atmosphere of worn elegance, though when the plaster began falling off the walls, and the doors off their hinges, not even another gin was sufficient to restore the ambience for some tastes. Too many of these wonderful old places were torn down and replaced by nondescript hotels. Some, however, have been restored and modernised without too much violence being done to their character.

CAIRO

With the Pyramids on its doorstep, the **Mena House Oberoi** enjoys one of the world's most spectacular locations. It began life as a khedival hunting lodge, becoming a hotel in 1869. This is now the old wing, magnificently decorated, where you can sit on the terrace of your suite with beautiful gardens below, and exchange stares with 5,000 years of history. It was here that Churchill and Roosevelt met during World War II to initiate plans for the Allies' D-Day invasion of Normandy.

The **Cairo Marriott Hotel**, or 'The Palace', was built by the Khedive Ismail in honour of the Empress Eugenie of France and her husband, who had been invited to attend the festivities for the opening of the Suez Canal in 1869. The central part of the hotel still retains its character, artefacts and decoration from that time, despite its modern use.

Early last century, Baedeker ranked Cairo's 3-star **Windsor Hotel** just below the old Shepheard's. Miraculously, the Windsor is still standing and it has not changed a bit. Its character is literally oozing through its walls, just as its mattresses sag heavily with the weight of history. Even if you do not stay here, you should visit its delightful bar-cum-lounge-cum-dining room, hung with weird curios and damaged paintings, a quaint setting in which to drink a beer.

ALEXANDRIA

If you stay at the **Cecil Hotel**, make sure you have a room commanding the magnificent view over the Eastern Harbour, where the Mediterranean splashes against the Corniche. You will see the site of the Pharos on the breakwater in the distance, and off to the right on the Silsileh headland you can imagine the palace of the Ptolemies. If that is not enough, what other hotel can say that Cleopatra put the asp to her breast just outside their front door? A Moorish pile built in 1930, the Cecil figures often in Lawrence Durrell's *Alexandria Quartet*. Ask to see the visitors' book.

LUXOR

In Luxor, the heyday of early 20th-century leisured travel is represented by the **Old Winter Palace**. At the rear, the rooms overlook the gardens, while the Nile flows by at the front. King Farouk's suite was over the main entrance. Any of the other rooms overlooking the Theban necropolis and the Valley of the Kings have good views.

ASWÂN

If you saw the film of Agatha Christie's *Death on the Nile*, you will recall Aswân's **Old Cataract Hotel**, probably the loveliest place to stay in all Egypt. Built in 1902, it is a period delight overlooking the southern tip of Elephantine Island. Its highlight is the terrace, an unforgettable place to sit while the sun is setting, watching *feluccas* flit like swallows in the Nile below. Sometimes the terrace is restricted to guests of the hotel only.

CAIRO

Mena House Oberoi,
Sharia al-Ahram, Giza. *Tel: (202) 3833222*;
e-mail: obmhogm@oberoi.com.eg;
www.oberoihotels.com
Marriott Hotel,
Saraya el Gezira, Zamalek. *Tel: (202) 7283000*;
e-mail: marriott@hotmail.com
Windsor Hotel,
19 Sharia Alfi Bey. *Tel: (202) 5915277*,
www.windsorcairo.com

ALEXANDRIA

Cecil Hotel,
Midan Sa'ad Zaghoul. *Tel: (203) 4807055*;
e-mail: h1726@accor-hotels.com

LUXOR

Old Winter Palace,
Sharia el Nil. *Tel: (2095) 2380422*.
e-mail: H1661@accor-hotels.com

ASWÂN

Old Cataract Hotel,
Sharia Abtal el Tahrir. *Tel: (2097) 2316000*;
e-mail: H1666@accor-hotels.com

The view from the Mena House Oberoi

On business

Volumes could be written on matters of law, finance and taxation as affecting business; suffice to say that visitors contemplating entering into a contract in Egypt, investing in the country or establishing a business there, should first make enquiries in their home country with government departments, their bank, their legal advisor and others, as appropriate, and with the Egyptian embassy there. In Egypt they should contact the commercial affairs section of their own embassy. Most countries have embassies in Cairo, and consulates in Alexandria (see p179).

Business facilities

Most 5-star hotels have business centres which provide secretarial and translation services – usually for both guests and visitors. They will also do photocopying, send and receive faxes, etc. You can use their computer facilities and hold small meetings. There are also numerous internet cafés throughout Egypt, in all major cities and towns.

Additionally, the courier service, DHL, is represented in all major cities in Egypt, and can ship business documents, gifts or holiday purchases home. Further information from their head office in Mohandessin, which is open 24 hours a day. All other branches are open 9am–5pm.
16 Lebanon St, Mohandessin.
Tel: (202) 3029801.

Business hours

Most businesses run their working day from 9am to 5pm Sunday to Thursday, closing Friday and Saturday. Government offices usually close around 1pm on Thursdays, all day on Fridays and some also close on Saturdays. Foreign embassies are closed on Fridays, the Moslem day of rest, and most on Saturdays too. During the month of Ramadan, business hours will be reduced.

Conference and exhibition centres

All Cairo's big 5-star hotels offer conference and/or exhibition facilities, with the Marriott, the Grand Hyatt, the Semiramis Inter-Continental and the Mena House Oberoi being the most popular. Large-scale exhibitions are generally held at the Cairo International Conference Centre. *Nasr Road, Nasr City. Tel: (202) 2634637.*

Customs

Customs regulations permit the free import of all personal effects, whether used or new, including such items as word processors and recorders. Nor is there any restriction on the amount of money you bring into the country.

Etiquette

Personal relationships are an essential part of Egyptian business life and a face-to-face discussion is always preferable to the telephone. At business meetings smart clothing should be worn. Business entertainment is invariably conducted at restaurants rather than at home, and generally without the involvement of spouses. Decision-making here is a slow process. Exercise patience.

Media

One initial, if somewhat thin, source of useful information is the daily English-language newspaper *The Egyptian Gazette* (on Saturdays it is called *The Egyptian Mail*). For greater depth there is the *Al-Ahram Weekly*, an offshoot of Egypt's distinguished daily newspaper, published every Thursday in English. There are also a couple of publications which will provide important phone numbers, contacts and resource lists, including *Business Today, Insight Magazine, Community Times* and *Egypt Today*.

To keep abreast of events generally, European newspapers are usually available in Egypt the following day, and the major international current affairs magazines are widely distributed, at a price.

Radio and TV

On any radio with a medium-wave-band, you can tune in to the BBC World Service, which broadcasts on 639KHz from 8.45am to noon, 3pm to 5pm, and from 7pm to 9pm; it also broadcasts on 1393KHz from 9pm to 3am. Five-star hotels pipe CNN and other television news and satellite services straight into your room.

Egyptian radio has English-language news broadcasts on 95FM at 7.30am, 2.30pm and 8pm, while Egyptian television's Second Channel presents an English-language news programme at 8pm.

Visas

If you are not actually running a business within the country but are simply making a business trip, there is no reason why you should not simply state 'tourism' as your reason for visiting, in which case the visa details as described in the **Practical Guide** section will apply (*see p176*).

New meets old in the cityscape of Cairo

Practical guide

Arriving

Entry formalities

Almost all visitors to Egypt require a visa and a passport still valid for at least six months. Tourist visas can be obtained in person (usually in 24 hours) or by post (allow between four and eight weeks) from an Egyptian consulate abroad, preferably in your own country. You can also obtain a visa on arrival at Cairo, Luxor, Sharm el Sheikh and Hurghada airports, and at the port of Alexandria. Single-entry and multiple-entry (three-visit) visas each permit you to stay a maximum of one month within three months of application. You can extend your visa for a month while in Egypt. Hotels will take a photocopy of your passport for registration purposes. On escorted tours registration is normally seen to by the tour manager.

By air

International flights arrive into Cairo, Aswân, Luxor, Sharm el Sheikh and Hurghada. Immigration procedure is straightforward, but queues can be long. Some travel companies do have charter flights to Egypt. Cairo airport has duty-free shops in the arrival and departure lounges. See Customs regulations (*p178*). You should remember to confirm your flight 72 hours before departure.
For flight information: tel: (202) 2675882/2675842.

To and from the airport

It is possible to get a public bus (No 949 from Terminals 1 and 2, and minibus No 27 from Terminal 1). These take one hour between Cairo Airport (Matar el Qahira) and Midan el Tahrir in central Cairo. It is preferable, however, for reasons of convenience, comfort and speed, to take a limousine or a taxi. The journey time is about half an hour. Limousines form a rank right outside and will charge at least LE100 into Cairo, more towards the Pyramids. Cheaper taxis lurk beyond; the important thing is to agree to a price in advance. Returning to the airport also involves bargaining, but the price will usually be lower, around LE60–LE70.

There is also a bus service from the airport to Alexandria. The journey takes about 3½ hours. Enquire at the SuperJet bus counter within the arrivals hall.

By sea

There are no longer any regular ferry services to Egypt from Italy and Greece. Daily ferries run between Aqaba in Jordan and Nuweiba in Sinai.

By land

Bureaucracy prevents most people from entering by car, but a vehicle can be brought into Egypt for three months if you have an *international triptyque* or a *carnet de passage de douane* issued by the automobile club of the country where the car is registered.

Practical guide

Camping

The few organised campsites in Egypt are mostly along the coasts and, more often than not, are without shade or adequate facilities. Some hotels provide prepared tents and camp beds. Check with the local police before camping on beaches; it can be dangerous, as some beaches are mined. Desert camping is generally less of a problem, but you should still attempt to get permission first; any land which is near water almost certainly belongs to someone.

Children

Children are more susceptible than adults to changes in diet, dehydration, extremes of temperature and exposure to sun, so extra care should be taken. For general medical advice, consult your doctor before departure. Take sun block with you – it is expensive in Egypt.

Egyptians generally like children, but have a robust attitude towards them. Do not assume that the same safety measures apply in Egypt as at home; far from it. Small children who do not need a seat to themselves can travel free on buses and trains. Children under two travel free on planes, and up to the age of 12 pay half fare. (*See* Children pp156–7.)

WEATHER CONVERSION CHART

25.4mm = 1 inch
°F = 1.8 × °C + 32

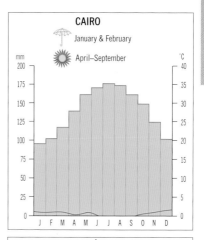

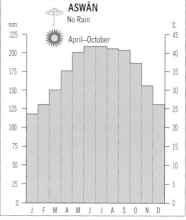

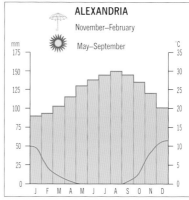

Climate

Average temperatures in Egypt can seem surprisingly low. Cairo averages 14°C (57°F) in January and 30°C (86°F) in August, but these figures mask considerable extremes between night and day temperatures, the result of the surrounding desert.

The coastal positions of Alexandria on the Mediterranean and, to a lesser extent, Hurghada on the Red Sea, reduce these extremes, and also give them a more even year-round temperature. As you move southwards, the air becomes drier and average temperatures increase.

Clothing

In winter you will need some woollens; in summer, light cottons will be most comfortable. In spring and autumn a combination of both is advisable against warm days and cool nights. In summer, at least one sweater is handy, as the deserts can be really cool as soon as the sun goes down. Alexandria has strong sea breezes. Take warm clothes if planning to sleep outdoors in winter (such as on a *felucca*). Clothes should be light in colour to reflect the sun and be easily washable and drip-dry. Bring comfortable walking shoes. Allow for conservative standards of dress. Wear trousers rather than shorts, skirts that fall to the knee, shirts and blouses that cover the shoulders and upper arms.

Convoys

Please note that you may be required to travel in a convoy from and to certain areas in Egypt, or have a police escort. Check with tourist information for details.

Coptic monasteries

Permission is not required to visit most monasteries in Egypt (*see pp66–7*). All are open to both men and women, but neither sex should wear revealing clothes. The monasteries do not have set hours for visiting, but because of dawn and evening prayers it is best to visit between 9am and 4pm.

A monastery may forbid entry to all or part of its enclosure during fast days. To confirm details of openings you should enquire first at the Coptic Patriarchate, Cathedral of St Mark, 222 Sharia Ramses, Abbassia, Cairo (*tel: (202) 6825374/5*). Check here too if you wish to stay overnight at a monastery.

The Greek Orthodox St Catherine's Monastery is closed on Fridays and Sundays, but is open to visitors from 9am to noon. Staying overnight is not permitted. Do dress conservatively.

Crime

You and your possessions are generally safe in Egypt. Nevertheless, take special care with passports, tickets and money. Hotels will look after your valuables for you, but you should obtain a receipt.

Customs regulations

All personal effects are exempt from duty. If you are asked to list these on a customs declaration form, make sure you leave with what you brought in, or you may be charged duty. If you lose anything, report it to the police and get them to give you written confirmation (you will also need this for insurance). You are also free to bring in any amount of foreign currency. Video cameras must be declared and registered in passports. On departure, the stamp in your passport will be cancelled.

You are permitted to bring in one litre (1^3/4pt) of alcohol, plus 200 cigarettes or 250g (8^3/4oz) of tobacco or 25 cigars free of duty. There are duty-free shops at Cairo Airport if you need to top up your supply.

The export of antiquities or any item over 100 years old without a licence is strictly forbidden.

Driving

To hire a car you must have a driving licence and be between 25 and 70 years of age. Car hire is expensive, but petrol is cheap. Both international and local companies operate in Egypt. Hertz and Budget have desks at Cairo Airport and offices in Cairo; most major hotels in Cairo and Alexandria have agency desks.

Third-party insurance is compulsory (make sure that it is included). Check the vehicle thoroughly before driving away, and make a note of any damage.

There are plenty of petrol stations in the cities, but they can be few and far between on the open road, so always try to keep your tank topped up.

Your main problem will be other traffic. Cairo is a madhouse on wheels, while country roads are busy with trucks, donkeys and camels. Traffic drives on the right, although you would not immediately guess it; drivers commonly ignore rules. Avoid driving at night; vehicles do not always bother to use lights, or drivers beam them into your face.

Hiring a car with a driver will not cost much more than self-drive. Or consider hiring a taxi for a half-day or day, agreeing on destination and price first.

Drugs

Do not bring drugs into the country or use any while there. Possession is a serious offence, while smuggling and dealing involves mandatory sentences of either life imprisonment or death. If carrying prescribed drugs, get a doctor's letter, just in case you are stopped.

Electricity

Electrical current is 220 volts AC. Sockets take the standard continental European round two-pronged plug.

Embassies and consulates

The following is an abbreviated list of embassies and consulates in Cairo. A complete list can be found in the *Cairo A–Z* and *Cairo: A Practical Guide*, two widely available local publications.

Some countries also maintain consulates in both Alexandria and in Port Said.

Language

The language of Egypt is Arabic. Its alphabet differs from that of Western languages, making phonetic transliteration difficult. English is taught to every school child, so you will probably find yourself widely understood. Nevertheless, here are some helpful basics.

BASICS

Yes	aywa or nam
No	la
Please	minfadlak
	(if addressing a man)
	minfadlik
	(if addressing a woman)
Thank you	shukran
No thank you	la shukran
You're welcome	ahlan wa sahlan
Sorry	asif
Good	kuwayyis
Bad	mish kuwayyis
God willing	inshallah
What?	matha?
I don't know	la adree

GREETINGS

Welcome	ahlan wa sahlan
(response)	ahlan bik
Hello (formal)	assalaamu aleikum
(response)	wa aleikum assalaam
Hello (informal)	saeeda
Good morning	sabah el kheir
Good afternoon	masa el kheir
Goodbye	ma salaama

CALENDAR

Today	innaharda
Tomorrow	bukra
Yesterday	imbarrih
Day	youm
Week	usbua
Month	shahr
Year	sana
Sunday	youm il ahad
Monday	youm il itnayn
Tuesday	youm it talaat
Wednesday	youm il arbah
Thursday	youm il khamees
Friday	youm il gumah
Saturday	youm is sabt

NUMBERS

0	sifr	14	arbahtarsha
1	wahad	15	khamastarsha
2	itnayn	16	sittarsha
3	talaata	17	sabahtarsha
4	arbah	18	tamantarsha
5	khamsa	19	tisahtarsha
6	sitta	20	ahshreen
7	sabah	21	wahad waahshreen
8	tamanya	30	talaateen
9	tesah	100	miyya
10	ahshara	500	khamsa miyya
11	hidarsha	1000	alf
12	itnarsha		
13	talatarsha		

DIRECTIONS

Where is Hotel ...?	feyn funduk il ...?
Where is the bank?	feyn il bank?
Where is the bus station?	feyn mahattat il autobees?
Where is the train station?	feyn mahattat il atr?
Where is the airport?	feyn il mataar?
Where is the restaurant?	feyn il matam?
Where is the toilet?	feyn il twalet?
Left/right/straight ahead	shimaal/yimeen/alatool

REQUESTS & SHOPPING

There is/is there?	fi/fi?
I (do not) want	(mish) aayiz (if you are male);
	(mish) ayza (if you are female)
How much?	bekaam?
It is too expensive	da ghaali awi
Bigger/smaller	akbar/asghar

REMARKS

I understand	afham
Do you understand?	hal tafham?
I do not understand	ana mish fahem (if you are male);
	ana mish fahma (if you are female)
Do you speak English?	hal tatakalam al-engleeziyya?
I don't speak Arabic	ana la atakallam
I speak a little Arabic	atakalam al arabiyya qalillan
Can you ... please?	hal taqdar an ... min fadlik
– speak more slowly	– mumkin tatakallam biboat?
– repeat that	– mumkin tukarir tilka?
I am tired/unwell	ana taaban (if you are male);
	ana taabana (if you are female)
I am (not) married	ana (mish) mitgawwiz (if you are male);
	ana (mish) mitgawwisa (if you are female)
Go away	imshee
Never mind	maalesh
Impossible	mish mumkin
Leave me	sebne
Excuse me	laow samat

Australia Cairo Plaza Tower, 1097 Corniche el Nil, Boulaq. *Tel: (202) 5750444.*
Canada 5 El Saraya Kobra Square, Garden City. *Tel: (202) 7943110.*
Ireland 3 Abu el Feda Tower, north of the Zamalek Bridge, Zamalek. *Tel: (202) 7358264.*
New Zealand Consular affairs are handled by the UK.
UK 7 Sharia Ahmed Raghab, Garden City. *Tel: (202) 7940850.*
US 5 Sharia America Latina, Garden City. *Tel: (202) 7973300.*

Egyptian embassies abroad

Australia 1 Darwin Avenue, Yarralumla, Canberra. *Tel: (06) 7234437.*
Canada 454 Laurier Avenue East, Ottawa, Ontario K1P 5P4. *Tel: (613) 234 4931.*
UK 75 South Audley Street, London. *Tel: (020) 7499 2401.*
US 2300 Decatur Plaza NW, Washington DC 20008. *Tel: (202) 234 3903.*

Emergency telephone numbers

The following are Cairo numbers.
Emergency (general): *123*
Ambulance: *(202) 123*
Fire brigade: *180*
Police: *122*
Tourist police (general): *126*
Tourist police: *Tourist Police (General) (202) 3688281/5904827 (downtown); 3834520 (Pyramids).*
Please note: Some staff will have limited or no English.

Glossary

Abu: holy man or saint, whether Muslim or Christian.
Ankh: the hieroglyphic sign for life.
Bab: gate.
Bayt: house.
Cartouche: in hieroglyphics, the oval band enclosing the god's or pharaoh's name and symbolising continuity.
Copt: a Christian of the native Egyptian Church.
Corniche: seafront or riverfront road.
Deir: monastery.
Fellahin: Egyptian peasants; the singular is *fellah.*
Harem: the private family (or the women's) quarter in a house.
Hypostyle: a hypostyle hall is any chamber whose ceiling is supported by columns or pillars.
Iconostasis: in a church, the altar screen to which icons are attached.
Ka: in ancient Egypt, the spirit believed to inhabit the body during life.
Khan: an inn built around a courtyard for travelling merchants and their animals. Also called an *okel* or *wakala.*
Khedive: viceroy (Mohammed Ali and his descendants ruled Egypt as the nominal viceroys of the Ottoman sultan until World War I, whereafter they ruled as kings).
Madrasa: a mosque serving as a theological school.
Mashrabiyya: wooden screenwork, often used in windows.
Mausoleum: domed tomb chamber.
Midan: a square.
Mihrab: a mosque's wall niche

indicating the direction of Mecca.

Minbar: the pulpit in a mosque.

Moulid: anniversary celebration of a Muslim or Christian holy person.

Muezzin: the person who makes the call to prayer from a minaret.

Naos: the sanctuary of a temple.

Narthex: a church's entrance vestibule.

Pylon: monumental temple gateway.

Sharia: street.

Health

No inoculation or vaccination certificates are required for entry into Egypt unless you are arriving from an infected area. Your doctor, however, may recommend precautions against yellow fever, cholera, typhoid, hepatitis A, tetanus and polio. Malaria is both seasonal and regional; check with your doctor before you go, and if you do need a prophylaxis, take it.

Bites of all kinds need the immediate attention of a doctor. Inflammation of the eyes can be indicative of trachoma, while contact with stagnant water can cause bilharzia; the former should be dealt with immediately, the latter can await a check-up at a tropical diseases hospital at home. Do not swim in lakes, rivers or streams, as these are sure places for picking up water-borne diseases. Your hotel, embassy or any pharmacist can recommend a doctor, most of whom will speak English or French.

In an emergency, the following private hospitals in Cairo are best. However, it is likely that you will need to hand over a cash payment or at least a substantial deposit in advance.

Al Salam Hospital

Syria St, Mohandessin.

Tel: (202) 3029091 or 3030501.

As Salam International Hospital

Corniche el Nil, Maadi.

Tel: (202) 5240250/5240077.

You may well suffer a brief upset stomach, a normal reaction to a change of diet and climate which passes after a few days. Eat plain food and drink a lot, but if it lasts too long, consult a doctor. There is no need to stop eating Egyptian food if you feel well enough to eat at all. Your system, used to the microbes back home, will adjust to the local variety. Standard preparations for stomach upsets are available at pharmacies.

While eating in Egypt be scrupulously hygienic. Make sure your food has been properly washed and prepared. If in doubt, avoid salads and ice cream and stick to hot dishes. Although drinking water is heavily chlorinated and theoretically safe, stick to bottled mineral water.

Remember that the sun can be hot at any time of year, and the temperature can fall off sharply at night. During the day you should wear a head covering and sunglasses. It is not advisable to drink spirits before sundown as this causes dehydration, nor to consume iced drinks during the heat of the day.

A high-factor suntan lotion is advisable, especially if you are in the desert. Insect repellent is very useful.

Hitchhiking

You will be expected to pay for a ride. Lone women should not hitchhike.

Insurance

You should take out personal travel insurance before leaving. It should give adequate cover for medical expenses, loss and theft, personal liability (but liability arising from motor accidents is not usually included – see below) and cancellation expenses. Always read the conditions, any exclusions, and details of cover, and check cover is adequate.

Report any losses or thefts to the tourist police immediately, and get an officially stamped statement, without which most insurance companies will refuse to pay claims money.

If you hire a car, collision insurance, often called collision damage waiver or CDW, is normally offered by the hirer, and is usually compulsory. You may be covered by your normal policy. If not, CDW is payable locally and may be as much as 50 per cent of the hiring fee. Neither CDW nor your personal travel insurance will protect you for liability arising out of an accident in a hire car if, for example, you damage another vehicle or injure someone. If you are likely to hire a car, you should obtain extra cover from your travel agent or other insurer before departure. Few private cars are insured in Egypt.

Media

English-language publications are *The Egyptian Gazette* (or *The Egyptian Mail* on Saturdays), the fortnightly *Cairo Times*, *Al-Ahram Weekly* (Thursdays), and the monthly magazines *Egypt Today* and *Community Times*. There is daily television news in English at 8pm on Channel 2, and the Nile TV Channel 9 also broadcasts in English. Satellite channels broadcast 24 hours a day.

Money matters

The Egyptian pound (LE) is divided into 100 piastres (PT). Notes are for 10, 25 and 50 piastres, and 1, 5, 10, 20, 50 and 100 pounds. Egyptian currency can be purchased abroad. Banks have exchange counters at Cairo Airport and major hotels. Thomas Cook and American Express also change money.

Major brands of traveller's cheques, such as Thomas Cook, denominated in sterling or US dollars, are generally accepted at exchange counters, banks and major hotels and shops. Credit and charge cards such as MasterCard, VISA and American Express are accepted at major hotels and shops. Always keep your receipts for exchange transactions.

Banks are generally open from 8.30am–2pm Sunday to Thursday. If you need to transfer money quickly, use the MoneyGram^SM Money to Egypt Transfer service. For more details call Freephone 0800 897198 (UK).

National holidays

Banks and offices will be closed on:
1 January New Year's Day
25 April Liberation Day
1 May Labour Day

23 July Revolution Day
6 October Forces Day
23 October Suez Day
23 December Victory Day

There are also many religious holidays, both Islamic and Christian. The most important of the holidays is Ramadan, the month of fasting, during which working hours are often shortened.

Opening hours

Department stores and shops are usually open from 9am to 1pm and from 5pm to 8pm or later (9am to 7pm in winter), though in tourist areas some shops may remain open all day. Some shops close on Fridays, most on Sundays.

During the month of Ramadan, shop hours are likely to be from 10.30am to 3.30pm and 8pm to 10pm or even later. (*For bank hours, see* Money matters.)

Organised tours

Tour operators offer a wide choice of package tours and cruises to Egypt, many including all transport, accommodation and sightseeing.

Thomas Cook, Abercrombie & Kent, Kuoni, Hayes & Jarvis and **Swan Hellenic** are among the leading names in tours and cruises (*see p162*).

Also very helpful is the Egyptian state agency **Misr Travel**, with offices in London, New York and Sydney. Their head office in **Cairo** is at 1 Sharia Talaat Harb, PO Box 1000. *Tel: (202) 483 1358.*
Australia Level 5, 630 George St, Sydney, NSW 2000. *Tel: (612) 9267 6979.*
UK Rooms 201–204, Langham House, 308 Regent St, London W1R 5AL. *Tel: (020) 7255 1087.*
US Suite 555, 630 5th Ave, New York, NY 10111. *Tel: (212) 582 921011.*

Pharmacies

Pharmacies in Egypt carry a full range of medicines, including many foreign brand names. They also often provide medicines available abroad only on prescription. Pharmacists are highly trained and can make helpful recommendations; they can also refer you to English-speaking doctors.

The Necropolis at Thebes

Photography

International brands of film are available in all tourist areas, though the range is limited. Always check the date on the package. Memory cards for digital photography can be purchased but it is better to bring your own supply. Do not photograph airports, bridges, docks, railway stations, government buildings or anything else of a security-sensitive nature. At the very least, you may find your film confiscated.

Places of worship

There are Protestant, Catholic, Greek Orthodox and Coptic churches, and also Jewish synagogues in Cairo and Alexandria. Places of worship in Cairo: **All Saints' Cathedral** (Anglican and Episcopalian) at Sharia el Gezirah, Zamalek. *Tel: (202) 7368391.*
Church of the Holy Family (Catholic),

55 Sharia 15, Maadi. *Tel: (202) 3582004.*
Jewish Synagogue Sharia Adli.

Police

See Emergency Telephone Numbers, *p182*, and Security, *p30*.

Post offices

The post between Egypt and abroad can be very efficient provided you use a postbox at a major hotel or in a central location, or you go to a post office. Some postboxes appear to be visited very rarely, if at all. In Cairo, the Central Post Office is at Midan el Ataba, near the Ezbekieh Gardens, and is open 24 hours daily. Other post offices are open 8.30am to 3pm daily, except Fridays. Most hotels can provide you with stamps for letters and postcards and will undertake to post them for you.

An unusual cargo, even in Egypt

Public transport

Air

EgyptAir, the state airline, operates frequent daily flights between Cairo and the main tourist destinations of Luxor, Aswân, Abu Simbel, Sharm el Sheikh and Hurghada. With less frequency it serves Alexandria, Matrouh, St Catherine's, El Kharga Oasis and the New Valley. There are also several small charter companies operating within the country. Always try to make reservations, especially to Upper Egypt and St Catherine's, as far in advance as possible.

Bus

Long-distance buses can be fast, cheap and comfortable. Bookings must be made in person at the relevant terminals, which in Cairo are:

To Alexandria and **Matrouh:** SuperJet service from Cairo Airport; El Mazha – Abu Bakr St, opposite EgyptAir Hospital in Heliopolis; Abdel Moneim Riad St near the Ramses Hilton and Midan Giza – Morad St, by Misr Petrol Station near the Cairo Sheraton.

To Hurghada and **Sharm El Sheikh:** SuperJet service from El Torgoman, behind *Al-Ahram* newspaper building and El Mazha – address as above.

To Port Said: Superjet service from 194 Ramses Street, near the train station.

To Ismailia, Suez, Hurghada, Sharm, Dahab, Nuweiba, Taba, Ras Sidr, St Catherine's, El Arish and **Rafah:** East Delta bus service from El Mazha – address as above, El Kolaly – El Galaa

CONVERSION TABLE

FROM	TO	MULTIPLY BY
Inches	Centimetres	2.54
Feet	Metres	0.3048
Yards	Metres	0.9144
Miles	Kilometres	1.6090
Acres	Hectares	0.4047
Gallons	Litres	4.5460
Ounces	Grams	28.35
Pounds	Grams	453.6
Pounds	Kilograms	0.4536
Tons	Tonnes	1.0160

To convert back, for example from centimetres to inches, divide by the number in the third column.

MEN'S SUITS

UK	36	38	40	42	44	46	48
Rest of Europe	46	48	50	52	54	56	58
USA	36	38	40	42	44	46	48

DRESS SIZES

UK	8	10	12	14	16	18
France	36	38	40	42	44	46
Italy	38	40	42	44	46	48
Rest of Europe		34	36	38	40	42	44
USA	6	8	10	12	14	16

MEN'S SHIRTS

UK	14	14.5	15	15.5	16	16.5	17
Rest of Europe		36	37	38 39/40 41	42	43
USA	14	14.5	15	15.5	16	16.5	17

MEN'S SHOES

UK	7	7.5	8.5	9.5	10.5	11
Rest of Europe		41	42	43	44	45	46
USA	8	8.5	9.5	10.5	11.5	12

WOMEN'S SHOES

UK	4.5	5	5.5	6	6.5	7
Rest of Europe	38	38	39	39	40	41
USA	6	6.5	7	7.5	8	8.5

St, Ramses; El Torgoman – behind *Al-Ahram* newspaper building.

To Sharm and **Suez only:** East Delta bus service from Crossroads of Abbassiya and Salah Salem roads.

To Luxor, **Aswân** and **Oases:** Wageh Ibly Bus Company: No designated stops (*tel: (202) 5760261 for pick-up information*). SuperJet: El MazAa (*tel: (202) 2909017*); El Torgoman (*tel: (202) 5798181*); A Moneim Riad (*tel: (202) 5751313*); Midan Giza (*tel: (202) 5725032*); East Delta (*tel: (202) 4198533*).

Let phone ring, but often there will be no answer.

Rail
Ramses Station (Mahattat Ramses), Midan Ramses, is Cairo's main train station. From here there are trains north into the Delta and Alexandria, south into Upper Egypt, and Wagons-Lits sleepers to Upper Egypt. The fastest trains take 2 hours to Alexandria, 11 hours to Luxor, and 15 hours to Aswân. Be sure they are air-conditioned. Full timetable details are in the *Thomas Cook Overseas Timetable* (published bi-monthly, obtainable from UK branches of Thomas Cook or by telephoning (*01733*) *416477*). For Upper Egypt, book a day in advance; for Wagons-Lits a week in advance. All services must be booked at Ramses Station (*tel: (202) 5753555*).

Local transport
City buses in Cairo and also trams in Alexandria are generally to be avoided as they are almost always jammed solid. However, Cairo has a very clean, efficient, and easy-to-use metro system.

Taxis are inexpensive. Rarely will one operate on a meter, and drivers will usually ask for LE10 from a foreigner for almost any journey in Cairo or Alexandria. In fact, LE5 will usually be enough. Carriages are a pleasant alternative, especially in Luxor.

Student and youth travel
Museums and sites usually offer a 50 per cent discount to students. Some discount is available on travel, though it is limited. Generally avoid youth hostels.

Sustainable tourism
Thomas Cook is a strong advocate of ethical and fairly traded tourism and believes that the travel experience should be as good for the places visited as it is for the people who visit them. That's why we firmly support The Travel Foundation, a charity that develops solutions to help improve and protect holiday destinations, their environment, traditions and culture. To find out what you can do to make a positive difference to the places you travel to and the people who live there, please visit *www.thetravelfoundation.org.uk*

Telephones
Cairo telephone numbers may well change soon with the addition of a 1, 2, 3 or 4 in front of the number. Dates for the change are stll uncertain at the time of writing. Local and international

telephone services are available in most hotels. Local calls can also be made from some kiosks, shops and restaurants. International calls can be made from PTT offices.

For assistance, dial *10.*

International dialling codes include:

Australia: *61* **Canada:** *1*
Ireland: *353* **New Zealand:** *64*
UK: *44* **USA:** *1*

Thomas Cook

There are Thomas Cook branches throughout Egypt, including:
Alexandria: 15 Saad Zaghloul St, Alexandria. *Tel: (203) 034847830.*
Aswân: 59, Abtal El Tahrir-Cornish El Nil, Aswân. *Tel: (2097) 2304011.*
Cairo: 17 Mahmoud Bassiouny St, Tahrer Square, Cairo. *Tel: (202) 5743955.*
Hurqhada: 3 Nasr St, Dakar. *Tel: (2065) 3451870.*
Luxor: New Winter Palace Hotel, Luxor. *Tel: (2095) 2372402.*
Sharm El Sheikh: Gafy Mall, Gafy Land, Sharm el Sheikh 56111. *Tel: (069) 3601808/9.*

Thomas Cook's website, *www. thomascook.com*, provides up-to-the-minute details of Thomas Cook's services.

Time

Egypt is two hours ahead of Greenwich Mean Time.

Tipping

See Baksheesh, *p25.*

Toilets

Apart from in the better hotels and restaurants, toilets can be off-putting. Never count on there being toilet paper. Squirters are sometimes provided, or a bucket of water with which you are expected to splash yourself.

Tourist offices in Egypt

Cairo: There are Tourist Information Offices at Cairo International Airport Old Terminal (*tel: (202) 4183132*) and New Terminal (*tel: (202) 2652482*), Terminal 3 (*tel: (202) 2653872*), at the downtown head office, 5 Sharia Adli (*tel: (202) 3913454*), and at the Pyramids (*tel: (202) 3838823*). **Alexandria:** The Tourist Information Office is in Midan Sa'ad Zaghlul (*tel: (203) 3932712*). In both Luxor and Aswân offices are centrally located on the corniche.

Websites

www.egyptembassy.com
Useful site for visa details and booking holidays.
www.touregypt.net
General tourist guide with information on activity holidays.

Travellers with disabilities

Few concessions are made to travellers with disabilities. However, most tombs and temples are accessible to wheelchairs, including the tomb of Ramses VI in the Valley of the Kings, the Citadel, the Museum, and major mosques in Cairo. Sandy sites like Saqqâra may be difficult to access.

Index

Acknowledgements

Thomas Cook wishes to thank the photographers, picture libraries and other organisations for the loan of the photographs reproduced in this book, to whom copyright in the photographs belongs.

EGYPTIAN STATE TOURIST OFFICE 85, 87, 147
FLICKR/Kodak Agfa 23, Checco 88, J Winfred 97, Tim Proffitt-White 121, photobradd 126, Sally Payne 151, 173, antoioperezrio 154, 186, Templar1307 155, D hess 157, Spkewerx 162, Rita Willaert 163
PICTURES COLOUR LIBRARY 20, 39, 43, 61, 92, 106
THOMAS COOK TOUR OPERATIONS LTD 21. 25, 27, 60, 75, 77, 81, 113, 119, 128, 137, 143, 160, 161, 168, 170, 171
WORLD PICTURES/PHOTOSHOT 1, 7, 41, 74, 82, 83, 185
The remaining pictures are held in the AA PHOTO LIBRARY and were taken by RICK STRANGE. Rick Strange would like to thank WINGS TOURS & NILE CRUISES for its help

Proofreading: JAN McCANN for CAMBRIDGE PUBLISHING MANAGEMENT LTD

SEND YOUR THOUGHTS TO
BOOKS@THOMASCOOK.COM

We're committed to providing the very best up-to-date information in our travel guides and constantly strive to make them as useful as they can be. You can help us to improve future editions by letting us have your feedback. If you've made a wonderful discovery on your travels that we don't already feature, if you'd like to inform us about recent changes to anything that we do include, or if you simply want to let us know your thoughts about this guidebook and how we can make it even better – we'd love to hear from you.

Send us ideas, discoveries and recommendations today and then look out for your valuable input in the next edition of this title.

Emails to the above address, or letters to Travellers Project Editor, Thomas Cook Publishing, PO Box 227, Coningsby Road, Peterborough PE3 8SB, UK.

Please don't forget to let us know which title your feedback refers to!